German Fighter Ace Erich Hartmann

GERMAN FIGHTER ACE
Erich Hartmann

Photo Selection & Commentary by Ursula Hartmann
Introduction by Manfred Jäger

Translated from the German by James C. Cable

The Life Story of the World's Highest Scoring Ace

SCHIFFER MILITARY HISTORY
West Chester, PA

Dust Jacket Artwork by Jerry Crandall, Sedona, AZ
Courtesy of Eagle Editions Ltd.
Prints Available through Eagle Editions Ltd.,
P.O. Box 1830, Sedona, AZ 86336

The Painting: THE KNIGHT AT DAWN
The reorganization of the Luftwaffe's Fighter *Gruppen* in the fall of 1944 resulted in 4th *Staffel* JG 52 transferring to JG 3, thus 7th *Staffel* at JG 52 replaced 4th *Staffel* into the II *Gruppe* and used the 4th *Staffel*'s small white numbering system.

During October 1944, Erich Hartmann was given command of the 7th *Staffel* and was utilized as part time *Gruppenkommandeur*. At this time they were based in Hungary.

The Aircraft
Of all the known aircraft flown by Erich Hartmann, this Messerschmitt Bf 109 G-6 was, in my opinion, the most colorful. The standard camouflage of the three grays, 74, 75, 76 appear to have been modified by over-spray, possibly of 76 gray. Note the black scallop design is different than the 109 G-6 flown by Hartmann in February 1945 when with JG 53. Also note the absence of the D-F loop antenna from the machine. Contrary to other renderings of this aircraft, it is strongly felt that it had the yellow under the cowling as did most 109's at this time.

- Jerry Crandall

Translated from the German by James C. Cable.

Printed in the United States of America.
ISBN: 0-88740-396-4

This book was originally published under the title,
Der Jagdflieger Erich Hartmann,
by Motorbuch Verlag, Stuttgart.

We are interested in hearing from authors with book ideas on related topics. We are also looking for good photographs in the military history area. We will copy your photos and credit you should your materials be used in a future Schiffer project.

Published by Schiffer Publishing, Ltd.
1469 Morstein Road
West Chester, Pennsylvania 19380
Please write for a free catalog.
This book may be purchased from the publisher.
Please include $2.00 postage.
Try your bookstore first.

Contents

We live in an age in which maximum performances are consumed like a product (and one also has the impression that they are produced in much the same way).

Then what does it mean that, not much more that a generation ago, a man came out of a war as the victor in 352 aerial dogfights? Even today this man's former enemies are still amazed by this. At first, they did not want to believe the numbers, because they seemed too fantastic. When they verified them and determined them to be valid, they faced a new phenomenon: was this man a product of the Hitler-state, of the "master race"? Obviously not, because they discovered a fair-haired lad who did not enjoy the inflexible military lifestyle; a 22-year old who taught himself concentration, who utilized clear judgement and quick reaction, who remained modest and reserved in victory; a warrior who, in ten and one half years of Soviet captivity, surpassed himself in the most difficult tests of human character; a man who also could become unpleasant when the truth was unpleasant.

And so there are a large number of former war-time enemies, among others, who are proud to be friends of the man named Erich Hartmann.

His life began on April 19, 1922 in Wiessfach, not far from Stuttgart. His father was a young doctor. Erich's life was already quite adventurous in his early childhood. A cousin of Erich's father, while on a visit to his homeland — at the time he was consul in Shanghai — advised the doctor to leave the inflation, food shortages, political and economic chaos behind him and come to China. Wanderlust tempted the doctor, he went to China and remained there.

He opened his practice in the city of Changsha on the Xiang, a tributary of the mighty Yangtzee Kiang river. He was the only white doctor in the city and was held in high regard and well paid by the Chinese. This allowed his wife and two boys Erich and Alfred to later follow him.

There was a beautiful island which stood in the middle of the Xiang river, which the Doctor liked very much. He quickly purchased it and had a house built there. For the children, the little island empire was a playing paradise which imposed no limits on childhood fantasy. It still haunts the dreams of the grown man today. . .

But the idyllic life in the far east was not to last. Revolutionary slogans and attacks against the "foreign Devil" became increasingly stronger. The foreigners lost their extra-

Photo opposite:
Messerschmitt Bf 109
high above the clouds.

territorial rights. Up until this point, the Germans remained unmolested due to a lack of cause for conflict.

After Dr. Hartmann made his way into the city one morning and recognized the severed heads of his English friends perched atop fenceposts along the road, he took the only logical step. He sent his wife and children back to Germany via the Trans-Siberian Railroad.

All week long they were shaken about on their journey. In Moscow, the train was to have a stop-over for one hour. Frau Hartmann wanted to utilize the time to obtain some food for the journey. She said to the two of them "You sit quietly. Erich, watch over Alfred. I'll come right back and bring you something to eat and drink." Then she disappeared into the chaos of the train station. Only when the train started up again without their mother being there did the boys become uneasy. Alfred started to cry, and Erich tried to quiet him and told him to stop his bawling. Their fellow passengers tried to determine what the matter was, but at the time the boys spoke a little Chinese, but not a word of Russian, and that led to even more confusion. The train rattled on.

After a seemingly terribly long time, the compartment door opened from the outside — while the train was moving — and in swung their mother, windblown hair and all. The first reaction of six-year-old Erich was to explain to his brother "You see? I told you not to cry so!" What had happened? After a long wait in the line at the kiosk, Frau Hartmann had just purchased the food when she heard the call for the train. Just then, a whistle sounded and she saw the train pulling away. She dropped everything and ran along the platform as the train went faster and faster. Just like in the old west — and almost completely exhausted — she was just able to grab the handrail of the last car and jump aboard. The Russian train consisted of railcars without passages between them. The individual cabin doors opened outward and one could enter them from the outside via a running board which ran along the entire length of the car. Frau Hartmann had to move hand over hand from one rattling railcar to the next, until she finally reached her children and was able to hold the frightened ones in her arms.

The episode may seem insignificant, but already the un-shakability which was to later distinguish him as a man was showing itself in the boy.

One half year later, the unrest in China had faded away and Dr. Hartmann wrote to his wife telling her she could return to

Changsha with the children. But the resolute young woman had had enough of the Far East and wrote to her husband: "I will not come back to China, but rather am looking for a medical practice in the area of Stuttgart where you can set up office!"

Dr. Hartmann returned to Germany and the family initially moved to an old farmhouse in the vicinity of Weil im Schönbuch. Three years later, there was a new house with a practice on Bismarkstrasse. With its roof, it bore a distant resemblance to a chinese pagoda. This is where Erich Hartmann spent the larger part of his youth before he went off to war.

Flying was his chief interest. An inclination toward the daring had made itself known, and thus it came to his first attempt at flying. He built a frame out of bamboo poles, spit, wire and some old blankets which looked like quite a creation. One day he made a running leap with this contraption off the balcony of his house. He made a hard landing in a ditch specially built for this purpose filled with soft, loose dirt, and remained unscathed. It must have been that this nine year-old took this possibility into account, why else would he have troubled with the digging of a ditch? A testimony to his sense of "calculated risk" — quite remarkable for his age!

The actual realization of his dream came in another way: his mother, herself a flying enthusiast, had joined the flying club at the Böblingen airfield, which was no more that ten kilometers from their house. After she received her private pilot's license for light aircraft, the family happily became passengers in a two-seat Klemm L 20. Unfortunately, the Klemm had to be sold during the course of the economic decline in 1932, but four years later Frau Hartmann founded a sailplane group in Weil and became the instructor for its young members. Erich was taken along every weekend to the meeting with the young members, and therefore was able to become an excellent licensed glider pilot at the age of 14. After being awarded the "C" license, he became a *Jungscharführer* in the *Flieger-HJ* (Hitler Youth Aviation).

Regarding school, this landed him in the *Nationalpolitische Erziehungsanstalt Rottweil* (the Rottweil National-Political Reformatory) where there was a military-like drill to provide for "discipline and cleanliness." It wasn't long before Erich came in conflict with this system. That is why Dr. Hartmann brought both of his sons to the *Internatsoberschule* school in

Korntal, where they allowed more freedom of personal development.

It was in Korntal where he met his future wife. At the time, he was 17 years old, and she 15. It was true young love, which withstood the attempts of the worried parents to counter it, and has lasted a lifetime. In April 1940, Erich Hartmann passed his university entrance examinations. In truth, he wanted to become a doctor like his father.

But war erupted in the meantime. The press and radio celebrated the successful fighter pilots, and it is not surprising that flying tempted him. Erich Hartmann joined the Luftwaffe (his father was less enthused). On March 15, 1940 he entered the *Ausbildungsregiment* (training regiment) 10 in Neukuhrn/Ostpreussen.

The time spent in Rottweil had awakened a antipathy toward the military tone and parade drill. Now he was forced to swallow this bitter pill because there was no other way to fulfill his dream. But blind obedience never was, and is still not, his strong suit, and this would later strongly influence the course of his life — not only during the war, but also in the new *Bundesluftwaffe*.

The flight training which followed basic training was quite a bit more peaceful and lasted two years (His father had hoped that the war would end in the meantime). Hartmann flew 17 different types of aircraft until finally becoming familiar with the one aircraft which was already enveloped in legend: the Messerschmitt Bf 109.

In his first attempt at aerial gunnery, he fired fifty rounds from the guns of his Bf 109D with the result of 24 hits on the tiny towed target. Those familiar with such things will realize what an excellent feat that is. On the March 31, he was promoted to *Leutnant*. The training had come to an end. The war was by no means over, as Hartmann's father had hoped, and Erich Hartmann was sent to the Eastern Front — to Jagdgeschwader 52.

He stood together with a pair of other new arrivals in the command bunker for the usual welcoming speech by the *Kommodore* (commander). But more than the words of *Major* Hrabak, an unusual event confronted him with stark reality.

Hrabak had just said: "In order to survive here and to be successful, the will to attack must be properly directed — with a level head, proper consideration and sense. Fly first with your head, and then with your muscles." At that moment, the

Kommodore's radio interrupted, "Clear the field! I've been hit. I have the field in sight and must land immediately!" The bunker sprang to life. And then the voice again, "Damn, I hope I can still make it. My engine is on fire!"

Everyone ran outside. The duty officer had just fired a red flare to clear the airfield. They could see a Bf 109 on approach trailing a thick black cloud of smoke. Its landing gear was down. The pilot got the plane under control, the aircraft sank down onto the grass strip and rolled a few meters.

Then something fell off the landing gear and flew away from the airplane. Burning and smoking, the aircraft broke to the left and somersaulted with a thunderous crash. "Man, that's Krupinski!" someone cried. The rescue crews raced out to extinguish the fire. Then the ammunition began to explode, 20mm shells and tracers shot out from the wreckage. Hartmann stood there unable to take his eyes from the fire. Suddenly, out of the chaos came order — the pilot ran out of the inferno into the open. It seemed a wonder that he was still alive. A *Sanka* truck brought him to the *Kommodore*. He was a strapping man, and he laughed as he approached Hrabak. "I was hit by a couple of pieces of flak over the damned Caucuses", he said. The new arrivals mouths were wide open in reverence. This, then, was the other side of the coin. Hartmann was assigned to the 7th *Staffel*. He knew that he could fly — his experience flying the glider had awakened in him a special feeling which had even saved his life on more than on occasion, when this "sixth sense" told him something was wrong with an airplane which he was flying, before it was reflected on its instruments. Now he wanted to get his first kill, quickly and surely. On his third flight as wingman to the experienced and proven *Feldwebel* Rossmann, there was enemy contact, and he made all the mistakes that only a newcomer can. As he tells it:

"Rossmann called out some enemy aircraft over the radio and started to dive. I followed. I myself could not recognize any enemy aircraft at first. As we leveled out at high speed, I discovered two dark green airplanes about 2000 meters in front of me and slightly higher. My first thought was 'I'm going to get one of them!' I gave full throttle and shot past my wingleader to get into firing position. I approached quickly and opened fire at about 300 meters. I noticed how my shots went past the target, high and to the left. The target in front of me became bigger so quickly, that I had to pull back on the stick and climb. I was immediately surrounded by dark green airplanes, which were turning in behind me. Now I was getting nervous. I had lost visual contact with my wing leader, climbed up through a cloud deck and was suddenly alone. Then Rossmann's came over the radio: "Never fear, I was watching you; I've lost you now. Come down through the cloud deck so I can see you again!

"I emerged from the cloud and saw an airplane at a range of about 1200 to 1500 meters coming directly toward me.

"I stared from fright and initiated a fast descent toward the west. I called my leader and reported that there was an unidentified aircraft on my tail. Rossmann's voice came back: 'Turn to the right so that I can come closer to you.' I turned to the right, but the plane on my tail cut the inside of my turn. I banked as hard as possible. Full throttle, descend to low-level flight and then off in a westerly direction. I could no longer hear Rossmann's words, pulled my head in behind the amour plating and waited for the crashing impact of enemy bullets in my airplane. The other plane was still behind me and after a while I heard Rossmann's voice again, who said to me that there was no longer an airplane behind me. I climbed to altitude to determine my position. To my left I saw the Elbrus river and could now find my way. Then I saw the red warning light for fuel light up. Five minutes later the engine went bong-bong-bong and stopped. I had no more fuel.

"Below me there were huge sunflower fields and a street on which a couple of trucks were driving. The ground came up quickly. I made a bellylanding in a violent cloud of dust, opened the canopy and took my personal gear out of the cockpit. Some army chums drove me the 30 kilometers back to Soldatskaya airfield.

"That evening, I received a loud bawling out by the *Gruppenkommandeur*, *Major* von Bonin, and then a lecture by Rossmann about *Rotten* (a flight of two aircraft) tactics, who presented me with my sins one my one:
1. Breaking from the wing leader without being ordered to.
2. Flying into the firing position of the wing leader.
3. Climbing through the cloud deck.
4. Confusing the wing leader with an enemy aircraft. (The "enemy" from which I dove away after descending through the clouds was Rossmann).
5. Failure to follow the order to assemble.
6. Lost orientation.

7. Loss of my aircraft without having inflicted damage upon the enemy.
I was grounded and was subordinated to the ground personnel for three days. I felt awful."

The first lesson Hartmann learned from this dramatic beginning on the Eastern Front was: don't repeat you mistakes. In the next two and one half weeks he flew as wingman and gradually got the feel for proper behavior in aerial combat. His chance came on November 5, 1942.

At about noon the *Schwarm* to which he was assigned was scrambled against 10 LaGG-3 fighter aircraft and 18 Il-2 fighter-bombers. The Russian formation obviously wanted to attack the German routes of advance. The German fighters spotted the enemy planes east of the city Digora. Hartmann recounts:

"Our position was above and behind our enemy. We divided the *Schwarm* into two *Rotten* and made a diving attack. We shot through the fighters and took a bead on the fighter-bombers. I attacked the aircraft on the very far left and closed in quickly and opened fire at a distance of 70 to 100 meters. The hits were good, but the bullets bounced off the Il-2. The heavy amour of this Il-2 even withstood hits from the 20mm cannon.

"During my second attack on the same aircraft I dove in and then approached it from behind and below. This time I flew even closer before opening fire and scored a hit in the oil cooler. Increasingly longer licks of flame leapt out of the black smoke which was pouring out if the Il-2. The fire streamed back under the fuselage. Now I was alone, because the airplane I attacked had separated itself from its formation in an attempt to escape to the east.

I stayed behind him, and we leveled off low. Then something exploded in the Russian's wing, and at the same moment, there was a violent noise in my plane. Smoke poured into my cockpit, and I saw flames in the engine cowling. There wasn't much time. I handled it like a training exercise. Present altitude: low-level flight behind German lines. So cut the throttle, close the main fuel valve and shut off the engine! This happened just in time. The plane was already sliding on its belly through a field, and whirled up a shower of dirt and dust which quickly put out the fire. As I was climbing out of the cockpit, my first victim crashed three kilometers away."

He quickly returned to his airfield. He had proven himself the better pilot in aerial combat and shot down an enemy — but also lost his own aircraft.

Two days later he had to be taken to the hospital with yellow fever. This meant a four-week rest. On January 27, 1943, he was able to shoot down a MiG and return safely. By the end of April the count was 11 shot down, among which was a "double": two LaGG-3's.

He overcame his "stage fright" and became more sure of himself, and developed his own combat methods. On July 7 he achieved 11 air victories on one day.

He flew constantly that summer, up to four sorties per day. And his nickname "Bubi" was spoken with ever-growing respect. By the end of August he had shot down 90 enemy aircraft. At the end of October it was 150. At the end of the war he was the all time leading fighter ace with 352 confirmed kills. The closest to come to him was Gerhard Barkhorn, with 301 victories. But it was not only the numerous opportunities which was the basis of his success. He got as close as possible to the other aircraft before opening fire — a throw-back to the ideas of Richthofen.

He himself said: "My entire tactic consisted of waiting until the opportunity to attack presented itself and then to attack with high speed. One must wait until the enemy fills the entire windscreen, and then not a single shot will miss! The further away one is from the enemy, the weaker the penetration power of the shots. With the tactics I used the enemy aircraft is hit with the full effect of the weapon. At such a short range your angle relative to the enemy simply does not matter, or if one is banking or flying some other particular maneuver. When the other plane is hit like this, he is going down. And you have even saved ammunition. This way, there is no problem of relative position or angle."

Hartmann knows the countless stories which are spread about his marksmanship, whenever the subject comes up. He dismisses such talk with the stroke of his hand and argues having had an admirable skill.

This may be another reason that everything worked out for him: that he never tried to kid anyone nor let himself be kidded. He was always certain of himself, even during times of bad luck, and made his decisions accordingly. It was August 20, 1943. The Russians had broken through at Donezbecken. The *Geschwader* was flying 24-hour operations to keep the skies cleared of Russian fighter-bombers.

During his first sortie, Hartmann had shot down an Il-2 and was pursuing another. At a range of 50 meters, he pressed the firing buttons to fire from all guns. The *Sturmovik* sank, broke up and was suddenly engulfed in flames. Hartmann passed closely above the Il-2 as he disengaged and searched out his next target.

Under his aircraft fuselage there were a couple of bangs, sounding much like backfires. Hartmann saw part of the engine cowling fly away and disappear behind him in the slipstream. He can still see every detail: choking blue smoke penetrating the cockpit. The first reaction was: gain ground toward the west! Because he knew that he was over Russian held territory. But then he had to throttle down, switch the ignition to the "off" position and close the fuel line — otherwise he wouldn't come down in one piece. He made straight for a large field of sunflowers and set down lightly, jolting to a stop with a metallic clatter. He unbuckled the parachute and prepared to climb out of the damaged plane. While he was laboring to get the on board clock out of its bent casing — because it had to be recovered according to standing orders — through his dust-covered windscreen he saw a German truck approaching. He was relieved, because in the unclear situation of the front, is was difficult to tell which areas were German and which were Russian at any given moment. As the truck came to a stop, he could see two hefty soldiers spring from the back. Shocked, he could see more clearly: the men were in foreign uniforms and had asian facial features. A cold sweat broke out on his brow. He knew that if he were to run, they would surely shoot at him. There was only one choice: fake an injury. As the two Red Army soldiers jumped up onto the wings and looked into the cockpit, he pretended to be unconscious. One of the Russian soldiers grabbed him under the arm and tried to pull him out. He screamed from "pain" and began to groan. The Russians let go of him and said good humoredly, "War over. Hitler 'kaputt.'" They had recently achieved a victory and were in a good mood. Hartmann pointed to his stomach and moaned. Through his half-closed eyelids he could see that the two soldiers had fallen for it. The Russians carefully helped him out of the airplane. Now it had become a real piece of theatre. He fell to the ground and appeared to not be able to stand. The Russians went back to the captured truck to get an old tent canvas and laid the "wounded" pilot on it.

They then carried him to the truck, put him in the truck bed and drove to their command post in a nearby village. A doctor appeared who could even speak a word or two of German, but Hartmann was even able to fool him (being the son of a doctor had paid off). His act lasted two hours. Then the same two soldiers returned and carried him out to the truck. As they drove off in an easterly direction, he realized he had to escape — and right away.

He assessed the situation. The truck had gone approximately three kilometers to the east. The one soldier drove, the other was in the back watching the "wounded German prisoner."

As he was considering some ideas, the characteristic wail of German Stukas could be heard coming out of the west. The truck began to slow down. The Russians wanted to be able to run for cover at any time. The Stukas made a low pass over them. As the guard was staring up at the sky, Hartmann jumped him. The Russian struck his head on the back of the cab and fell to the floor. This is his chance! He jumped over the tailgate and ran as fast as he could into a field of towering sunflowers next to the road.

He had hardly disappeared under their cover when the screeching of the trucks brakes indicated that his escape had been discovered. He ran deeper into the sunflowers, all the while hearing rifle shots behind him. Bullets whistled past him. Then the shooting became no more of a threat to him, but he maintained his pace for the next five minutes. Every step could mean his salvation. Coughing, he emerged from the sunflower field into a small valley which looked to have come right out of a fairy tale. A small stream splashed along peacefully between luscious green fields and flowers. A stark contrast to his life and death escape. But here he found the quiet to thoroughly analyze his situation and to come to a decision. After a short rest, he made his way toward the west. It must have been about nine in the morning. After half an hour he came to a street which led to a little village. He cautiously went around the village to a small hill from which he had a view. On the next rise he could see soldiers and trenches. The front could not be too far.

He resisted the urge to continue on during the daylight and went back to the stream, where he built an inconspicuous shelter out of sand and stones to keep himself from being seen. Then he laid down behind it and went to sleep. He awoke in the late afternoon and prepared to leave his camp. When dusk fell he went on his way. Artillery fire thundered through the night. Tracer bullets and flares etched their paths across the dark sky and indicated the course of the front. He reached the hilltop where the soldiers had been digging trenches earlier that day. The positions were empty. On the other side of the hill he entered more sunflower fields. He snaked his way through the flowers, constantly trying to move the flowers as little as possible. He repeatedly took rest breaks. In the tension he could forget the hunger which started when he flew off that morning without breakfast. After an hour he heard a noise. Squatting down, he observed a ten-man Russian patrol which was also snaking its way through the sunflowers. He estimated his chances and decided to follow the reconnaissance patrol — at a sensible distance, of course.

The Russians led him to the edge of the sunflower field. He took cover and watched as the soldiers crossed a field and passed by two houses. From his cover, he saw the patrol disappear into the darkness. Just then, concentrated machine gun fire ripped through the night. Hand grenades exploded. The remainder of the reconnaissance patrol appeared out of the darkness screaming and disappeared again into the sunflower field.

At this point, he estimated that his own lines must run along the next hill. He marched off, and as was nearing the hilltop, he whistled a German song. He did not want to get mowed down by a burst of machine gun fire. After a few minutes he stood atop the hill. There was no one there: no German comrades, no positions, no sign of life. His shoes struck against empty ammunition casings. This is where the firefight had been. He continued on toward the west through the night. It must have been midnight. For two hours he slipped and stumbled his way across the terrain. Then he came to another slope. The only thing he could hear was his own breathing. "Halt!" The unexpected cry in front of him was followed by the crack of a rifle fired at close range. He felt the bullet cut through his pantsleg. "Good God, don't shoot at your own people!", he shouted, shocked. "Halt, who's there?", came a second cry. Hardly 20 meters in front of him stood the guard who, thank God, narrowly missed him. "I am a German fighter pilot who was shot down. Don't shoot!", he called, "For God's sake, let me through!"

A sharp commanding voice said "Let him come." He walked toward this voice. The guard followed him and shoved the muzzle of the rifle in his back. And then he was behind German lines. . .

He had made it back. With intuition, clear assessment of the situation and self discipline. However, when Hartmann had not come back from his sortie and even his returning comrades could not testify to his fate, Hartmann's first mechanic was not satisfied. *Feldwebel* Mertens wanted to be certain. His comrades watched as he rolled up a blanket in his tent and stuffed food into a backpack.

"Where are you headed?", they asked him.

"I am going behind the Russian lines. To find my boss there. I'm going to get him."

"You'll be shot if they catch you."

"I speak Russian, the people will help me."

Mertens left without notifying anyone. He did not have permission to leave the airfield. He simply took a rifle and disappeared on foot in the direction of the front. If his boss were still alive, he wanted to find him and bring him back.

Now Hartmann had come back, but "Bimmel" Mertens was missing. The big worry faded on the next day, when the unmistakable upright form of *Feldwebel* Mertens wandered back across the airfield. Dark circles were around "Bimmel"'s eyes and his cheeks were hollow. He was obviously near to breaking down. Then he saw Hartmann. A smile broke out across his gaunt face. The two men shook each other's hands with a silent expression of the kind of deep affection which bonds two men who are ready to lay down their lives for one another. Such closeness is valued by those men who are upright and truthful under all conditions.

Hartmann could not bear it that he was to lay down his pistol before entering Hitler's inner circle on the occasion of being decorated with the Diamonds to the Oak leaves with Swords of the Knights' Cross. His feeling was: "If Hitler doesn't trust me any more, then he can take the Diamonds and stick them." And he won out against the general order. This is how it came to be that this young fighter pilot entered wearing his weapon in the usual manner — despite the strict ban against wearing a pistol in Hitler's presence. He took it off when they drank coffee in the first conference room, but put it back on when he went with Hitler to dine in a nearby building.

This unbendable composure was what distinguished him in ten and one half years as a prisoner of war in Russia. (So much so, that others found strength in his example.)

Erich Hartmann had climbed to the summit of his fame,

wore the highest honors, the love of his youth had become his bride, and he continued to be fortuitous. He could consider himself fortunate.

Then the war was over. Lost — as was expected. In the final hours a radio message arrived at the *Geschwader* in Deutsch-Brod: the *Kommodore, Oberstlt.* Graf and the *Kommodore* of the 1st *Gruppe, Major* Erich Hartmann, were to fly to Dortmund. The remaining personnel of JG 52 were to surrender to the Russians. The Commanding General of the *Fliegerkorps* had so ordered.

Graf thought: "The Russians will very likely put the two of us against a wall and shoot us right away."

Hartmann asked: "Then should we listen to this order from *General* Seidemann?"

The two men looked at the 2000 women, children and old people outside — relatives of *Geschwader* personnel, refugees from the Russians. And the two considered it treason to "run off" and abandon them.

But they did not want to fall into Russian hands so easily. American troops were already in Pisek — approximately 100 kilometers distant. They had to reach them. They could surrender to them.

And they were able to do it. But what they did not know was, according to the agreement of the victory powers, all persons who were taken prisoner by the Americans east of Pilsen, Czechoslovakia, were to be handed over to the advancing Russians. . . After eight days in prison, the group of personnel belonging to Graf and Hartmann were singled out and loaded onto trucks. It was said they were all being brought to Regensburg. After a few kilometers' drive, the truck convoy stopped. They had reached a field which was surrounded by Russian soldiers. The people were made to dismount the trucks. Even while the people were hesitatingly climbing down from the trucks, the Russians were separating the women from the men.

As they drove off, the American GI's were able to catch a glimpse of the nature of their allies. They had to witness unimaginable sorrow and gruesome acts, without being able to help.

The victory delirium of the excited Soviet soldiers raged just as the Soviet authors and propagandists had intended. The otherwise good-natured Russians knew no bounds of cruelty toward all the defenseless people, soldiers, refugees, women and children.

The excesses then ended just as suddenly as they had begun. A Russian general appeared on the scene and immediately recognized what was going on. He issued orders which made such cruelties punishable, and resorted to drastic measures when his order was first violated: without a trial or formal proceedings, the perpetrator, who had been identified by the victim, was hung before the eyes of his Russian comrades and the German prisoners.

Hartmann, who was barely 23 at the time, stood as one of these eye-witnesses and was shocked. And gradually the fear of an uncertain and dangerous future grew inside him.

This is the moment he swore to himself not to give in to apathy and resignation, but to do all he could to survive - come what may.

What did come was ten and one half years of merciless isolation, during which time he became a symbol for many of his fellow prisoners, a symbol of unbroken resistance.

It started in the swampy Kirow camp, with hard labor, lack of nourishment and living in foxholes covered by some of branches. Later came the first attempts at psychological pressure in a better, almost "comfortable" camp. He was supposed to squeal. Become an informant. His refusal landed him in isolation in the "bunker." What kept him going was the thought of the wife he loved more than anything, and his small son whom he did not know, of whose birth he had only learned in camp. And this is precisely where his torturers started. The MWD, who controlled all prisoners of war, tried to find a soft spot in this unbendable man.

"You dirty fascist pig! Don't you know that you are completely in our power? Don't you know that your Germans are just dirt in the eyes of the rest of the world? Here in Russia we can do with you anything we like — anything. No one is concerned about what happens to you, Hartmann!"

The MWD officer shoved his pale face right up to Hartmann's. "What would you say if we, right here on a platter, were to bring you the heads of your wife and your young son?" Hartmann became pale. His stomach tensed and knotted. "Do you know that with the help of our East German friends we can pass unimpeded directly to Stuttgart to kidnap your wife and take her out of Germany? You know, of course, that we got to Trotski? And General Miller in Paris? We can get a hold of anyone we want, anywhere in the world." The bloodthirsty threat hit Hartmann where it hurt. But he could not let the MWD see the paralyzing fear which the threat had aroused. Hartmann looked directly at the officer and said, as quietly as he could: "You can do anything you want. You have the power to do so. I know that. But I will not work for you against my country and against my imprisoned comrades." Then the other officer slammed his fist on the table: "Dammit, Hartmann! Why don't you work for us? To Hell with you!"

Scenes such as this were to be repeated more or less regularly in a half dozen Soviet camps with at least 18 or 20 different MWD officers who threatened him with every conceivable idea. The persuasions ranged from wild blackmail attempts to offering him a commission in the East German air force. Hartmann's answer was always the same — no. (If his friends, co-workers and former commanding officers see a "somewhat pig-headed man" in him today, then they should remember how this attitude kept him going for a decade and preserved his self-respect.)

In an attempt to break the backbone of Erich Hartmann's morale, the MWD stopped his in-coming and out-going mail. Any details which could be extracted from his wife's letters were told to him in a heartless manner in order to break him. They only let him know just enough as to create an unbearable homesickness. Hartmann did not break down, but rather continued his resistance to the point of a hungerstrike. This led to forced feeding and solitary confinement — for 27 days. Then the *Kommissar* altered his tactics. He employed different weapons.

"Look, Hartmann, look here! I have five letters from your wife. Five letters. They are full of news from home and about your family. All you have to do is stop the hungerstrike and you'll get the letters."

For two years he had heard nothing from home, and now there were five signs of life — within his reach.

At this moment Hartmann knew that he was at the end. But once again he refused to sign the damned paper. Only at the next session of forced feeding did he say "I'll feed myself again. I am stopping my hungerstrike." The *Kommissar* brought his five letters. After Hartmann had read them for the third time, the *Kommissar* reappeared, pulled a paper out of his pocket and laid it on the table together with a fountain pen.

"You must sign this", he said.

Hartmann quickly scanned the standard compilation of

charges which he was to acknowledge with his signature: he had murdered women and children, destroyed property and inflicted severe materiel losses on the Soviet Union.

Hartmann knew that his wife was well. Now was able to endure everything again. He shoved the paper back. "I have read my mail. Therefore, I needn't admit to these lies."

The Russian made a thoughtful face and said, "I'm warning you, Hartmann. You will never be released from prison." In following weeks, more than two thirds of the inmates of the Kuteynikovo prison were repatriated. After the departure of the last truck, the *Kommissar* appeared with a squad of armed soldiers and went through the barracks. A sergeant called for quiet.

The *Kommissar* climbed atop a bench and read a declaration of the Soviet Government. One-sided polemics, intolerable accusations of supposed brutal murders of Russian women and children, destruction of Russian property and other accusations. Then came the reading of a long list of names, one of which was: Erich Hartmann, *Major, Deutsche Luftwaffe*.

And then the bombshell.

". . . all the above-named German prisoners of war are, from this day forward, classified as war criminals by order of the Soviet Government and Soviet law. From now on, these prisoners shall not be afforded the protection guaranteed by the Geneva Convention and the International Red Cross. They will now be dealt with as criminals according to Soviet law. All the above named war criminals are hereby sentenced to 25 years forced labor."

The *Kommissar* had made his threat against Hartmann come true. The few trials which followed were nothing but a farce. Weeks later, the news about the sentencing appeared in the Stuttgart press. Uschi Hartmann read the news at the breakfast table. Her mother came over to her. Uschi managed a sad smile.

"I'll wait for him, mother. I will wait. . ."

Hartmann then was placed in the Shachtu work camp. He again refused to work and cited the Geneva Convention. And again he was put into solitary confinement. News of this brought the situation in the camp to a boil. As his fellow prisoners were returning from work on the fifth day of his confinement and saw through the bars how two stocky guards were trying to force-feed him by pulling his hair and violently forcing his mouth open, they became completely enraged.

When reveille was sounded the next morning, an angry cry arose from hundreds of throats. Before they really knew what they were doing, the furious prisoners ran out of the barracks and overpowered their guards. A mutinous riot poured across the courtyard to the duty office of the commander.

Hartmann hadn't noticed any of this from the darkness of the bunker and was surprised when he heard heavy blows being driven against the bunker doors. Someone yelled "We'll get you out!" Axes cut a hole in the door so that someone could put his hand through it. Then the lock was open. Two fellow prisoners stumbled into the bunker breathing heavily. They shouted, "We detained the entire camp staff. You are free, Bubi. It's a real revolt." They cut his shackles and helped him to his feet.

As Hartmann arrived in the duty office of the commander, he noticed the large mass of prisoners which had gathered in front of the building.

The Colonel, his two Majors and the woman doctor looked somewhat of a disgrace. Two German officers, *Oberst* Wolf and *Oberstlt*. Prager had played the main roles in motivating the rebellion. But now all the prisoners were looking to Hartmann and were expecting him to assume control. They had done it for him, after all.

The Russians in the camp command obviously thought they were about to forfeit their lives to the man for whom the prisoners had organized the revolt. They were mistaken.

"Let them go, all of them. And then leave them alone", said Hartmann.

It is his authority which kept the others from making an escape from the camp — an escape doomed to fail. He was able to convince them due to the weight of his personality and the fact that the General responsible for conditions in the camp had promised improvements. But he and his fellow officers Prager and Wolf were considered instigators of the unrest and he was put in a special secured camp where he was to spend five of the next nine months alone. There, in Novotsherkaask, he was tried by a special court consisting of a General, four Colonels two Majors and a secretary for "Inciting the population of Shachtu to a revolt" and sentenced to 25 years hard labor. The sentence had already been determined before the tribunal conducted its phoney trial. When Hartmann was brought to Diaterka in the Urals in 1953, the story of the uprising had become legendary and had long since preceded him. He was assigned to the platoon for "problematic" prisoners. But, in 1954 he was returned to the notorious prison of Novotsherkaask.

His mother had turned to Stalin and Molotov with petitions without getting the slightest reaction. In the meantime, the Federal Republic of Germany had regained a place on the world stage. Hartmann's mother turned to Chancellor Adenauer. He answered her letter personally and promised to take special measures — in the interest of all the other prisoners still held in Russia as well. He was true to his word. When he travelled to Moscow in order to conclude a general treaty and trade agreement with the Soviet Union, he made it clear that the release of former soldiers held for more than a decade was an inalterable prerequisite to the signing of the treaty. Erich Hartmann's name was on the list of those whose release the German government demanded.

When his train departed headed for his homeland, Hartmann, after ten years of unbroken resistance, was close to breaking down. He was going home. . . to Usch. . . !

He still could not believe it.

His father and small son had died while he was gone. What else had changed?

He returned to a world of unimaginable abundance. He wanted to build a life together with his wife, and to make up for all they had missed during the long years of his imprisonment. If the war had not come, if he had become a doctor like his father. This was still his desire. But he was a realist and could count. To begin a demanding course of medical study at age 33, even when all the signs are good, is an almost senseless ambition.

He faced other difficulties as well: for ten years he had been cut off from any kind of possibility for academic training or further education, and even his high school knowledge of chemistry and physics had long since faded into memory. He felt a yawning gap that the decade in prison had left behind, as far as any occupation is concerned. Age 33 was late to start in any career.

The rest can be told quickly: Old comrades who were now serving in the new Luftwaffe came to see him. Hartmann hesitated. But finally he said to himself: "Flying is all you know. That is the thing you are good at and have accomplished something in. Perhaps you should just forget that you cannot bear the military, just like you forgot in 1940 when you had the opportunity to become a pilot."

24

He was approached once again. His former *Kommodore* Dieter Hrabak came to him to personally voice a request for him to join the *Bundesluftwaffe*. There was a place for Hartmann there and a secure existence. Shortly after Hrabak came Hartmann's former school teacher Simpfendörfer, who was now Minister for Education and the Arts in the state government in Stuttgart. He was accompanied by a high official from the Ministry of Defense in Bonn. They explained to him that his reactivation would not only fulfill the wishes of his comrades but a political necessity as well.

Krupinski, Barkhorn and Rall called him from time to time or visited.

He was never promised Heaven on Earth, but he was offered a good career and material security.

In contrast to all these offers, attempts to get established in other areas were disappointingly unsuccessful. The months passed. He had to do something. The new Luftwaffe offered him his chance. In a field in which he had proven himself. During these critical months his wife said nothing which might have influenced him one way or another. It was to be his own free choice. When at the end of 1956 he decided to re-enter the Luftwaffe, she accepted that fact.

But even within the Luftwaffe there were differences of opinion about his future use. This controversy was to be typical of later problems which determined Hartmann's career. After a bureaucratic squabble Hartmann was commissioned as a *Major* (and not as a *Hauptmann*, as was originally intended), but there would be no shortage of things to trip him up along the way.

In his flying he found himself again quickly, and his jet aircraft training offered him no difficulties, as he had already flown the Me 262 during the war. He felt like new.

And speaking of new: on February 23, 1957 his wife gave birth to a new baby girl in Tübingen. Their joy was boundless. During the course of that year he was sent to advanced jet-fighter training in America. At the USAF Luke Air Force Base in Arizona, he trained under almost perfect weather conditions in gunnery, low-level attack, bombing and toss-bombing in the T-33 and F-84. There were more an more contacts with Americans, not only in the course of duty but also in his private life, who in many cases became long-term friends, particularly when he brought his wife to America to stay with friends for a short time. When they returned to Germany, this idyllic period came to an end about which Frau Hartmann says nostalgically: "It was the most wonderful time we ever had in our lives." Hartmann's stay in the U.S. was filled with official duties, but there also a more pleasant side: he was particularly interested in the F-104, the most advanced weapons system of its kind at the time. He drove to Nellis Air Force Base in Nevada, where there was a training squadron for the F-104. Officially, the American pilots were full of praise for the aircraft — speed, power, climbing ability, weapons. But when Hartmann visited with the same pilots after duty in the bar, he heard a different story.

He realized that the F-104's condition of flight readiness was rather poor. So he asked about the reasons for this. And then they related their daily experiences with the F-104.

They mentioned troubles with the engine, problems with the fuselage landing gear, regulation of the exhaust aperture and other things. When Hartmann spoke with the ground crews, the mechanics told him of problems they had in keeping the aircraft deployable and flight-ready. The catalogue of problems with replacement parts, equipment defects and maintenance problems was by no means inspirational.

Hartmann hadn't been sent to America to assess the F-104, but he was a professional pilot and, as a future *Geschwaderkommodore*, was keenly interested in the aircraft which he knew would be deployed in the NATO forces in the foreseeable future. A young Air Force Captain with whom he had become friends gave him a thick file containing all the results of accident investigations up until that time. Hartmann reviewed all of this technical evidence very carefully. He was convinced that the young German Luftwaffe still had much to learn and much more experience and know-how to gain before they would be ready for such and aircraft. This viewpoint was to later hurt him, despite it proving to have been accurate.

When he came back to Germany, he was offered the command of a *Jabo-Geschwader*. He declined because he did not see this as his only field of activity. He continued to maintain his position that he would wait for the first jet fighter squadron. This was to be established in Ahlhorn and be designated *JG71 Richthofen*. With the attention of *General* Kammhuber, then Inspector General of the Luftwaffe, a more "adventurous" part of his career as a flying officer began. He set up the new *Staffel*'s and preached the necessity of gaining flight experience, flight experience and flight experience. He knew that one day the F-104 would come. And he knew just how "hot" this plane was.

As a *Geschwaderkommodore* he made use of his combat experience. He did everything as if at war, "so that we don't get used to any bad habits." He did not concern himself with parades and roll calls. In his opinion, combat readiness was something far more important. He held the view that future conflicts would not allow time to get up to full combat readiness. His efforts were always for constant combat readiness. The German armed forces have good reason to adhere to this principle perhaps more than any other.

Hardly six months after Hartmann had begun with the establishment of the *Geschwader*, in October, *JG 71 Richthofen* was subordinated to NATO.

To achieve this level of performance other units needed at least a year. For a *Kommodore*, who was "not a good officer", this was an achievement which could not be surpassed by other units even ten years later.

His stance on the F-104 was to hurt him once again. He had spoken out to delay the procurement of the F-104.

General Kammhuber asked him why.

Hartmann said: "Sometimes I believe that we Germans are so hated in the world because we say 'We are Germans, we can do it!' We think that we will be able to master this complex weapons system. The next procurement from the Americans should be the F-100 and the F-102. These are the next generation of aircraft with which we can gain experience with afterburners and other technical advances. Only then can we introduce the F-104 with the corresponding knowledge and base of experience. But we should not buy any airplane we cannot yet cope with." Kammhuber answered in a friendly manner, and with some good advice: "Hartmann, never speak of that. We are lucky to be able to buy this airplane. The politicians have made the decision."

Hartmann's biography closes with the words: "If Hartmann had been the type of officer to fit in, the kind which got along well at this point in time in the Luftwaffe, he would have been happy with that. Unfortunately for him, he gave direct answers to people who asked him direct questions and he backed his opinions. Through the grapevine, his views about the F-104 made their way up to the high political circles and fueled the already wide-spread belief that he was not the man to be considered for special positions of leadership. That the F-104's fell from the sky, and in surprising numbers, did not change things for him. He had been tripped up. Investigations and four hearings resulted from bureaucratic trivialities. Even though he was acquitted, he was sent to a high-level staff position near Cologne. In mid-1968 at the energetic recommendation of the old battle wagon *General* Günter Rall, he was finally promoted to *Oberst*. On September 30 1970, Erich Hartmann voluntarily retired from active service. Not as a man who had survived his own legend, but as a man who preserved the measure for striking a proper balance in a time of changing values."*

Manfred Jäger

* Toliver/Constable, *Holt Hartmann vom Himmel*, from Motorbuch Verlag, Stuttgart.

APPEAL

The brutal 10 1/2 years of imprisonment have led Hartmann to consider how one can save other generations from such experiences. Because the possibility of future war seems greater to him than that of maintaining peace, Hartmann has put his thoughts into an appeal:

Subject: Prisoners of War
My appeal to the governments of the World:
1. No nation of the world engaged in hostilities should be permitted to maintain on its territory the prisoners it takes.
2. All nations of the world should agree, that during the war, all prisoners of war taken by the warring powers are to be held in a neutral state.
3. The neutral nation holding the prisoners of war should continue to hold them until the conflict is ended.
4. After the end of the hostilities the prisoners of war should be sent home as soon as possible. I raise this appeal because the practical experience of hundreds of thousands of affected men has shown, that the prisoner of war regulations of the Geneva Convention are no longer do justice to the actual conditions.

Erich Hartmann
10 1/2 years prisoner of war in the USSR

There's no need to make excuses for people when they talk about the great deeds of the best, because men of this generation were filled with a true love for their fatherland and saw their duty in the fight for their country and its existence, an honorable act just as it has been throughout the centuries. One should not attempt to glorify war; most of us have gotten to know it well enough on our own. Nevertheless, impressive performance in battle and showing bravery, courage and ability under difficult duty and personal commitment should be — on both sides — given the praise and recognition of all decent-minded people.

It is said, and to a degree rightly so, that in the retelling of aerial dogfights, the horror of war tends to be overlooked. The same can also be maintained about most of the heroic epics of world history. One must not forget that such accounts of outstanding acts grew from a tragedy of massive proportions. It cannot be denied that mankind has gone through war, time and again throughout history, and that there have been men in every war who fought bravely and spurred others on through their concept of duty and their bravery on the battlefield. Without such men, freedom would have been lost long ago. Perhaps even in World War II.

One may argue that the preservation of democracy could not have been fought for by both sides. This is also true. On the other hand, and above all, soldiers were fighting for their fatherland. The majority of the what must have been millions of soldiers in the Second World War carried in them the conviction of fighting for the just cause of their country. National propaganda, tainted news and the assertions of politicians (in Nazi Germany a controlled press and manipulated radio) were sufficient to create a believable picture for the average citizen, because it is seldom possible to see behind the scenes. Therefore, wars are not fought by citizens who have subscribed to a good and just cause which is impartially pleaded by their government, but by millions of people who are simply fighting for their country, and in so doing, believe and hope that their government is in the right, and that which they read and hear is the truth.

It is too much of a demand to expect of each man that he obtain an overview of the world, through his own research, insight and knowledge, which is fair to everyone. The statesmen and masses of people of the press and radio bear this responsibility and pay the price for it often enough.

THE VOICES OF ONE-TIME ENEMIES

When war begins, the average youth or man fights for his country because he sees it as his duty, or simply because the entire legal authority of the state stands behind the call-up. . ."

(from Edward H. Sims "Jagdflieger", Motorbuch Verlag Stuttgart, pages 33-34)

"In Hartmann's opinion, the worst sin of a fighter pilot is scoring a victory and, in so doing, losing your wingman. For him, no aerial victory was worth the life of a wingman. In his unit, he who returned after a victory without his wingman was no longer able to fly as a flight leader and himself must fly as a wingman.

Hartmann's fearless, direct way of tackling problems was evident on the occasion of being decorated with the Diamonds to the Oak Leaves with Swords, which took place in the *Führer*'s headquarters. It was shortly after the assassination attempt of July 20, 1944. No one was allowed to enter the third, inner zone without first being searched by the Officer of the Watch. Hartmann explained to the officer who demanded he take off his pistol that he could tell Hitler that he did not want the Diamonds "if the *Führer* doesn't trust his officers at the front." Hitler's *Luftwaffenadjutant, Oberst* von Below, then explained that Hartmann could enter the third zone without being searched and could even keep his pistol.

Hartmann's position was simple: Hitler can stick his Diamonds if he doesn't trust me. Hartmann was not and is still not the kind of man who keeps discomforting thoughts to himself. He openly expresses them and defends them fearlessly.

(from Toliver/Constable "Das waren die deutschen Jagdflieger-Asse 1939-1945", Motorbuch Verlag Stuttgart, pages 144 and 145)

Since his youth, open and direct, ill disposed to "diplomatic" solutions, but always striving to do the feasible, Erich Hartmann has made his way with camaraderie and modesty — critical in his judgement, sometimes unpleasant, occasionally uncompromising, but never wavering.

THE AIRCRAFT

The Messerschmitt Bf 109 was the most widely produced fighter of the Second World War — some 35,000 were produced in various production series. Erich Hartmann flew the "109" exclusively.

In use since the Spanish Civil War, this model improved by leaps and bounds with the widest of improvements and engine alterations, from 670 horsepower (hp) (in the Jumo 210 A engine), to 1475 hp (in the DB 605 A engine), from hardly 2000kg takeoff weight to 3600kg, induced by larger fuel tanks, heavier weapons and armor. The last series, G and K, are distinguished by their high-power engines and improved firepower.

The large drawing below depicts the Bf 109 G-14 (all-weather fighter). Measurements (all models shown are the same): wingspan 9.92m, length 8.80m, height 2.34m. Engine: 1475hp DB 605 AS. Unpressurized cockpit. Armament: two MG 131's and one MG 151/20; additionally there was a weapons nacelle (under the wings) with two MG 151/20's available. The model of the G-series was, due to its numerous bulges in the fuselage (particularly over the connections for the MG 131), lovingly nicknamed *"Beule"* (boil) or *"Bollenpest."*

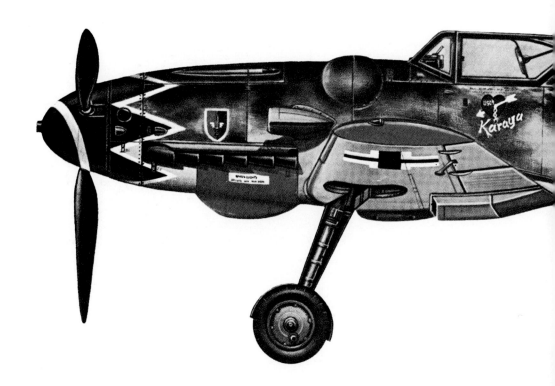

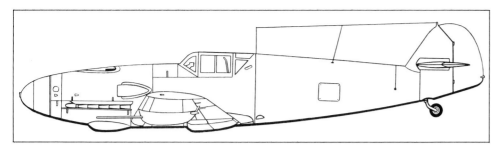

Bf 109 G-4
Fighter. Engine: 1475hp DB 605 A-1. Armament two MG 17 and one MG 151/20 (centrally firing through the engine); for enhancement cowling armament with two Mg 151/20's. Radio system: FuG 16 ZY. Pressurized cockpit. Max speed: 640 km/h at 7200 meters.

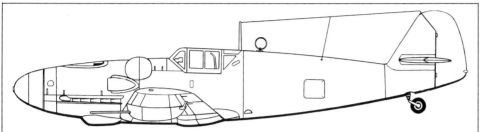

Bf 109 G-6
Fighter. Engine: 1475hp Db 605 AS. Armament two MG 131 and one engine-mounted MK 108 (30mm). Additional weapons nacelle possible. Radio system: FuG 16 ZY. Standard model without pressurized cockpit. Max speed 630 km/h at 7000 meters.

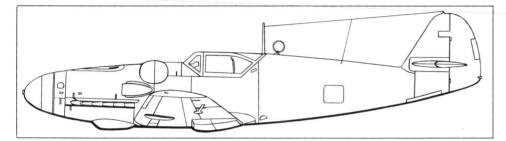

Bf 109 G-10
All-weather fighter. Engine: 1435hp DB 605 D. Standard armament two MG 131 and one MG 151/20. Without pressurization, but partially equipped with the "Galland-Haube", and wooden rudder. Radio system: FuG ZY, G-10/R 6 and additionally with a fighter radio navigation system.(main drawing caption)

Bf 109 G-14

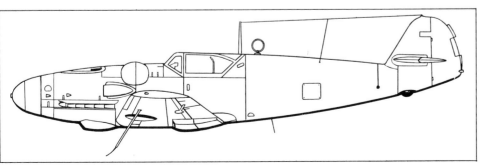

Bf 109 K-4
Fighter. Engine: 1435hp DB 605 D. Armament two MG 131 and one MG 151/20 or one MK 108. Radio system: FuG 16 ZY and FuG 25 A. Pressurized. Max speed: 680km/h at an altitude of 7600 meters. Takeoff weight 3400kg.

ENEMY AIRCRAFT

Polikarpov I-16 "Rata"
Fighter and fighter-bomber.
Wingspan 8.9m. Length 6.13m.
Height 1.70m. Single 1000hp M-62
radial engine. Crew: one. Max
speed: 505km/h. Armament two
20mm cannons, one 7.62mm
machine gun up to six rockets or
two 100kg bombs. Takeoff weight
1900kg.

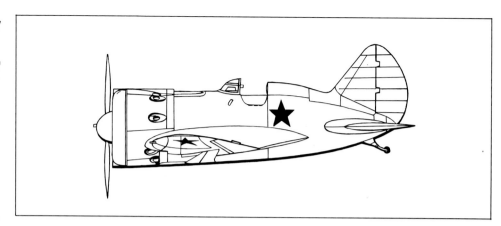

Polikarpov R-5
Multi-purpose biplane; light night
bomber. Wingspan 15.50m, length
10.56m, height 3.62m. One 500hp
V-12 M-17 engine (built under
BMW license). Crew: two. Max
speed: 230km/h. Armament two
7.62mm machine guns, up to
450kg of bombs. Takeoff weight
3350kg.

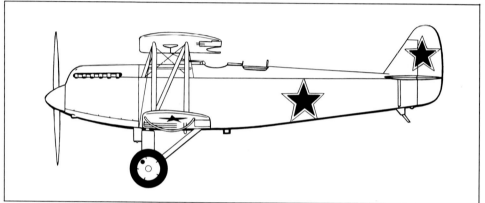

Polikarpov U-2
Multi-purpose biplane; light night
bomber ("*Rollbahnkrähe*").
Wingspan: 10.20m, length: 6.20m,
height 2.80m. One 160hp Shvetzov
M-11 five-cylinder radial engine.
Crew: one to two persons. Max
speed: 145km/h. Armament none.
Load: several small bombs.

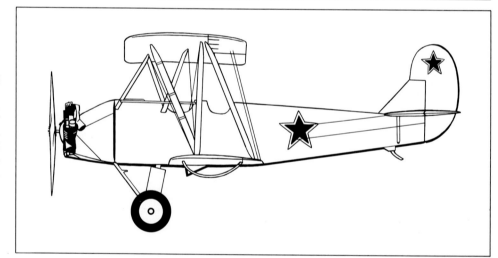

Mikoyan and Gurevitch MiG-1
Fighter and fighter-bomber.
Wingspan: 10.30m, length: 8.15m,
height 1.80m. One 1350hp Mikulin
AM-35 V-12 engine. Crew: one.
Max speed: 628km/h at 7200
meters. Armament one 12.7mm
machine gun, two 7.62mm
machine guns and up to 200kg of
bombs. Takeoff weight 3100kg.

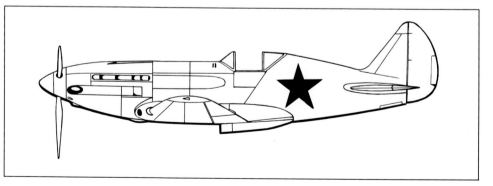

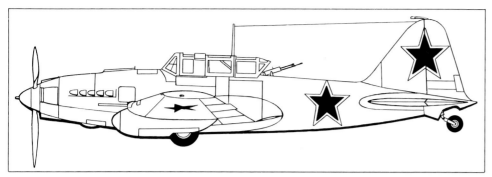

Ilyushin Il-2 "Sturmovik"
Attack aircraft, armored. Wingspan:
14.60m, length: 11.60m. One
1770hp Mikulin AM-38 V-12
engine. Crew: two. Max speed:
410km/h at 2000 meters.
Armament two 20mm cannons,
one 12.7mm machine gun, two
7.62mm machine guns, up to
400kg of bombs or eight 25.4kg
rockets. Maximum takeoff weight
5510kg.

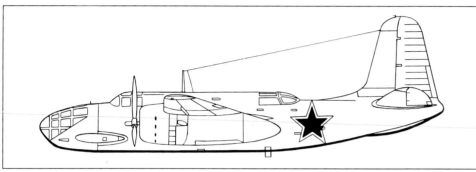

Douglas A-20 "Boston"
Bomber, delivered through Lend-
Lease. Wingspan: 18.77m, length:
14.60m, height: 5.18m. Two 1690hp
Double Cyclone twin-row radial
engines. Crew: three. Max speed:
510km/h at 3000 meters.
Armament nine 12.7mm machine
guns, up to 900kg of bombs as
external load. Maximum takeoff
weight 10,900kg.

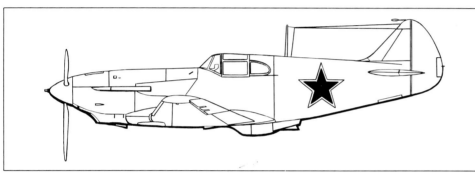

**Lavotchkin-Gorbunov-Gudkov
LaGG-3**
Fighter and fighter-bomber.
Wingspan: 9.78m, length: 8.88m,
height: 2.69m. One 1100hp Klimov
WK-105 V-12 engine. Crew: one.
Max speed: 556km/h at 5000
meters. Armament one 20mm
cannon, one 12.7mm cannon, two
7.62mm machine guns and up to
220kg of bombs or six rockets.
Maximum takeoff weight 3190kg.

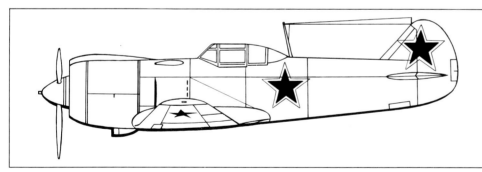

Lavotchkin La-5
Fighter and fighter-bomber.
Wingspan: 9.79m, length: 8.51m,
height: 2.81m One 1850hp
Shvetzov ASch-82 FN twin-row
radial engine. Crew: one.
Maximum speed: 644km/h at sea
level. Armament two 20mm
cannons, a choice of 150 bombs.
Maximum takeoff weight 3360kg.

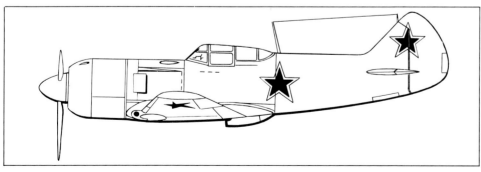

Lavotchkin La-7
Fighter and fighter-bomber.
Wingspan: 9.80m, length: 8.60m,
height: 2.75m. One 1775hp
Shvetzov ASch-82 twin-row radial
engine. Crew: one. Max speed:
653km/h at 6000 meters.
Armament three 20mm cannons.
Takeoff weight 3420kg.

Lavotchkin La-11
Fighter and fighter-bomber.
Wingspan: 9.80m, length: 866m,
height 2.80m. One 2100hp
Shvetzov ASch-70 twin-row radial
engine. Crew: one. Max speed:
674km/h at 6000 meters.
Armament three 23mm cannons.
Takeoff weight 3500kg.

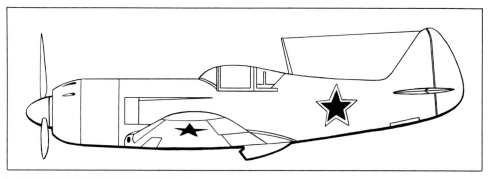

Yakovlev Yak-1
Fighter and fighter-bomber.
Wingspan: 10.00m, length: 8.47m,
height 1.70m. One 1100hp Klimov
WK-105 PA V-12 engine. Crew:
one. Max speed: 550km/h at 4000
meters. Armament one 20mm
cannon and two 12.7mm machine
guns. Maximum takeoff weight
3000kg.

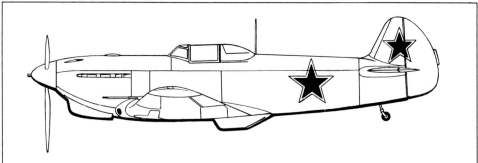

Yakovlev Yak-7
Fighter (later improved
aerodynamically and given a
bubble canopy). Wingspan:
10.00m, length: 8.47m, height
1.70m. One 1260hp Klimov WK-
105 PF V-12 engine. Crew: one.
Max speed: 520km/h near to the
ground. Armament one 20mm
cannon and two 12.7mm machine
guns. Maximum takeoff weight
3050kg. Range: 600km.

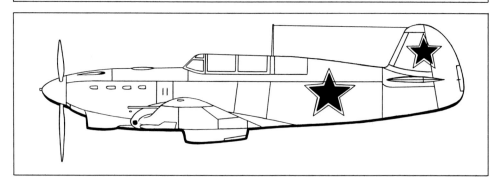

Yakovlev Yak-9
Escort fighter and fighter-bomber.
Most-produced Soviet aircraft of
the second world war. Wingspan:
10.00m, length: 8.50m, height
1.70m. One 1260hp Klimov WK-
105 PF V-12 engine, later a
1600hp M-107 A. Crew: one. Max
speed: 580-690km/h. Armament
one 12.7mm machine gun, one
20mm cannon. Maximum takeoff
weight 3060kg.

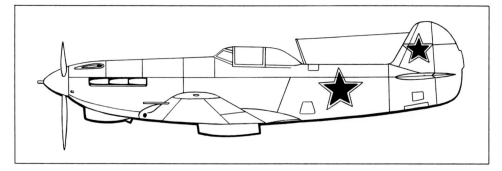

Petlyakov Pe-2
Dive-bomber for attacking point
targets (originally intended as a
high-altitude bomber). Wingspan:
17.16m, length: 12.66m, height
4.00m. Two 1260hp Klimov WK-
105 V-12 engine. Crew: three. Max
speed: 580km/h. Armament one
12.7mm machine gun, four 7.62mm
machine guns, up to 1000kg of
bombs. Takeoff weight 8250kg.

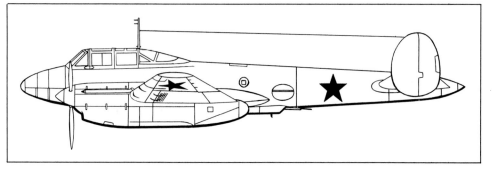

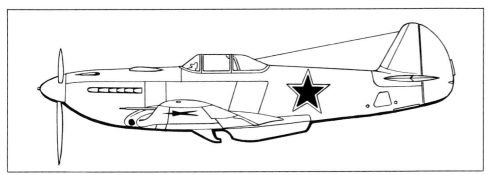

Yakovlev Yak-3
Fighter and low-level attack plane (developed from the Yak-9, but made lighter). Wingspan: 9.20m, length: 8.49m, height 2.38m. One 1260hp Klimov WK-105 V-12 engine. Crew: one. Max speed: 650km/h at 4000 meters. Armament: one 20mm cannon, two 12.7mm machine guns. Max takeoff weight 2650kg.

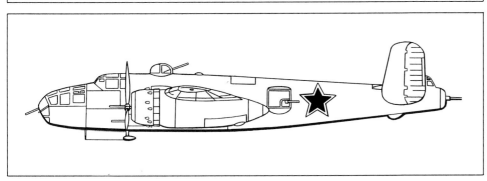

Bell P-39 "Aircobra"
Fighter and fighter-bomber. Delivered through "Lend-Lease."Wingspan: 10.38m, length: 9,20m, height 3.78m. One 1200hp Allison V-12 engine. Crew: one. Max speed: 617km/h. Armament one 37mm cannon and four 12.7mm machine guns. Takeoff weight 3765kg.

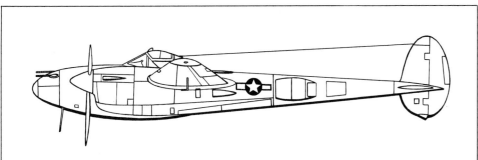

North American B-25 "Mitchell"
Medium weight bomber and low-level attack aircraft. Delivered through Lend Lease. Wingspan: 20.57m, length: 16.12m, height 4.80m. Two 1850hp Wright Cyclone twin-radial engines. Crew: six. Max speed: 440km/h. Armament up to 13 12.7mm machine guns, up to 1.8 tons of bombs. Maximum takeoff weight 15,200kg.

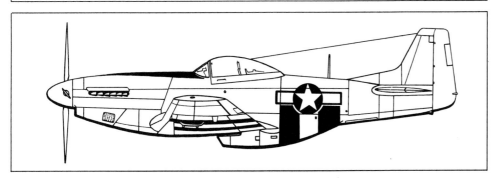

Lockheed P-38 "Lightning"
Long-range fighter and fighter-bomber; twin fuselage construction. Wingspan: 15.88m, length: 11.55m, height 2.99m. Two 1475hp Allison V-12 engines. Crew: one. Max speed: 664 km/h. Armament one 20mm cannon, four 12.7mm machine guns, up to 1.8 tons of bombs or 12.7cm rockets. Maximum takeoff weight 7950kg. Range: up to 3650km.

North American P-51D "Mustang"
Long-range escort fighter and low-level attack aircraft. Wingspan: 11.28m, length: 9.82m, height 4.16m. One 1490hp Rolls Royce/Packard Merlin V-12 engine. Crew: one. Max speed: 698km/h. Armament four or six 12.7mm machine guns, up to 900 kg of bombs. Maximum takeoff weight 5260kg.

Childhood and School Years

Weil im Schönbuch on an old postcard.

Weil im Schönbuch

. . . then, as today, an island of quiet and tranquility, and hardly cut off from the big wide world as one would like to think; the then well-known Böblingen airfield was hardly more than a couple of kilometers away; but the nearby provincial capitol of Stuttgart helped make the family house into a cosmopolitan home. It was a place where the world still seemed to be in order.

Hartmann's parents during their engagement in 1919. His father was born on 1 October 1894 in Ehingen/Donau, his mother on 16 February 1897 in Ebingen (Württemberg).

The house where Erich Hartmann was born in Weissach (Württemberg). It was a former parish house situated across from the town hall, previously Hauptstrasse 113, and now Hauptstrasse 14. The room where he was born was located over the main entrance, from which his mother is peeking. His father stands at the entrance. The door below on the right leads to his father's first medical office.

The house of his birth as seen today.

The family has begun.
Mother with brother
Alfred (1/2 year old) and
father with Erich (1 1/2
years).

Father Hartmann with
Erich, summer 1922.

Fifty years later . . . Erich
Hartmann stands at the
same spot.

Mother Hartmann with Erich, right, and Alfred, left, in July 1924 shortly before their departure to China. There was not all too much to prepare: only a small travelling bag for a trip halfway around the world.

12 September 1924: Departure from Germany. In the Hamburg harbor prior to embarkation — Erich holding his mother's hand.

Life on board the "Adolf v. Bayer." Mother Hartmann is the first woman on the right, Erich in front sitting on the deck, behind him his brother Alfred.

On the steamer "Adolf v. Bayer." Erich, right, on the Captain's arm.

Father with the language instructor in customary dress.

The new life of the family began in Changsha on a contributory of the mighty Yangtzee-Kiang. Alfred, left, Erich, right, with their mother.

Ride in a rickshaw. Erich, right and Alfred, left.

Nanny Zauma with Rolf Schnabel, from one of the families who were friends to the Hartmann's, and holding the hand of Alfred, right. Erich is with the nanny's son, squatting.

Lodgings with medical office in Changsha, China.

Dr. Hartmann, second from the right (with hat), with his Chinese patients in front of his office.

Father, center, with the Chinese language instructor, left. Mother is to the right, brother Alfred standing, Erich is on the ground playing.

Zauma, the Chinese language instructor.

The children Erich and Alfred playing chess — in their own way.

Chinese rice farmers at work — a picture of peace . . . yet the fires of unrest had already started.

Back home by way of the Trans-Siberian Railroad in 1928. Father opened his third practice in Weil im Schönbuch, a little spot south of Stuttgart. The photo shows the home, the former "zum Schwanen" inn on Hauptstrasse. There was no indoor plumbing in the area, which is why there is a well in the foreground. Father and Mother in front of the main entrance.

WEIL IM SCHÖNBUCH

An old aerial photo of Weil am Schönbuch with the new house.

The house built in 1932 at 9 Bismarkstrasse from a bird's-eye view.

First playmates in Weil im Schönbuch. From left to right: Erich, the two sons of the *Forstmeister* (or chief forest ranger), Reinhard and Walter Burger (both were later killed on the Russian Front).

Erich's nine and ten year-old friends in Weil. From right to left: Brother Alfred, Erich, son of the parish priest Eberhard Roller with a visiting guest, and the sons of the *Forstmeister* Reinhard and Walter Burger with a uest.

As 10 and 11 year-olds in the Weil im Schönbuch *Jungvolk* (a Hitlerian youth organization for 10-14 year-olds), Upper row, third from left is Erich, and bottom row second from left sits Alfred.

Like all boys at this age, Erich plays soldier.

Erich at age 10 next to the swimming pool in the garden.

Erich with his father in the swimming pool, sailing the washtub.

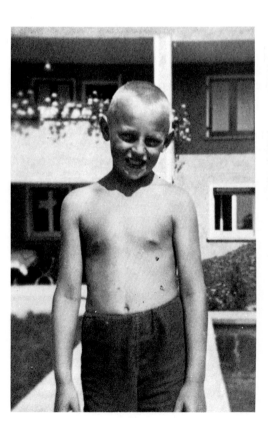

Prior to his first flight with
Mother and brother Alfred
on a Junkers airplane of
Lufthansa airlines from
Böblingen to Munich in
1928.

First contact with
Stuttgart's commercial
airport in Böblingen. The
new administration
building with air traffic
control tower.

Lufthansa aircraft of the
period, seen from the
terrace of the Böblingen
airport building.

Mother, shortly before her solo cross-country.

The famous Klemm-Daimler L 20 in flight, with Mother at the controls.

The sport aircraft of the Böblingen flying school.

Confirmation photo: Erich at 14, middle row, sixth from left, in front of the *Martinskirche*, (Martin's church) in Weil im Schönbuch, April 1936.

Erich as a member of the *Jungvolk* at the same age.

THE MOST DIFFICULT YEAR

The most difficult schoolyear for Erich: 1936 in the *NPEA* (National Political Reformatory) in Rottweil am Neckar. "Discipline and Cleanliness" was the motto.

The humble dining hall of the *NPEA*.

Erich in the institutional uniform of the *NPEA*. Free time was almost unheard of then.

Left, top to bottom:

The gameroom of the *NPEA*. Unfortunately, there was rarely enough time to play!

Pupils spent most of their time in the so-called work room.

The sleeping area of the *NPEA*, simple but clean. One bed and one chair were allotted to each boy of the institute, and they were always tired at night.

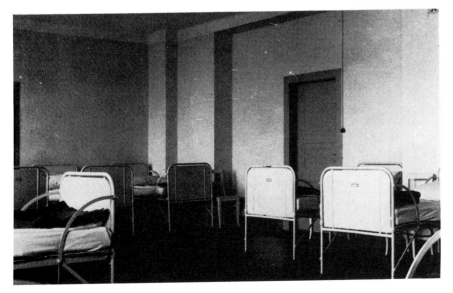

Roll call formations and marching were part of the every day life at the *NPEA*.

Erich with his schoolmates in their summer uniforms on a field trip. Erich is in front, sitting to the right. In the middle is the class teacher and the *Jungmannzugführer* (leader of a young men's platoon) Steck.

A field trip with *NPEA Rottweil* to Allgäu. Erich waving. His friend Fritz Stähle, with the walking stick, is a Captain with Lufthansa today.

The boarding school in Korntal where Erich escaped the ''Discipline and Cleanliness'' of the *NPEA* in 1937. Here he spent his best years of school. ''Understanding, decency and learning'' was the motto here.

THE OTHER SCHOOL

Prof. Kurt Busch (right), leader of the boarding school and a teacher, was very popular with the students and a good role model.

In the boarding school's work area, homework was completed under the supervision of one of the teachers. Erich, second from right.

Between physical
education and classes
there were leisure times.
Erich loved dizzying
heights even then and
enjoyed studying on a
chimney!

Here he performs a
headstand on this
uncomfortable spot!

Erich with his closest
school friend Wolfgang
Kürschner during a walk
in the spring sunshine.

A happy trio. Erich,
center, Wolfgang
Kürschner left, and to the
right is Helmut Wörner.

Leisurely tea with his mother, 1937.

. . . but he was more interested in sports than leisurely teas.

URKUNDE

Erich Hartmann B.b.3/427

errang beim

Bann= und

Untergau=Sporttreffen

in Leonberg

Schwimmen

400 m Kraul

im _____

den __1.__ Platz

Der Führer des Bannes 427 (Strohgäu):

Brunner

Erich Hartmann

errang im

100 m Kraul

den **1. Sieg**

mit der Leistung von **1 Min. 24 Sek.**

In Anerkennung der Leistung
verleihe ich diese Auszeichnung

LEONBERG, DEN 30. JUNI 1940

DER K.-FÜHRER DES BANNES STROHGÄU (427)

[signature]

The first place certificates in swimming from his Korntal school days are proof of his athletic ability.

Erich shows his ability with a 1 1/2 somersault from the three meter board.

Hard work rewarded.

Urkunde

Erich Hartmann

erkämpfte sich bei den

Skimeisterschaften 1940

des

Bannes und Untergaues Strohgäu

den 1. Platz

im Abfahrtslauf

Der A. Führer des Bannes 127

Leonberg, Februar 1940

Erich achieved his
summit in skiing
during the ski
championships in
1940 in Oberstaufen.
Erich on the right with
the number 49, and
his friend Fritz Stehle
next to him with
number 52.

Urkunde

Erich Hartmann

erkämpfte sich bei den

Skimeisterschaften 1940
des
Bannes und Untergaues Strohgäu

den **2.** Platz
im **Kombination**

Der K.-Führer des Bannes 427

Leonberg, Februar 1940

Urkunde

Erich Hartmann

erkämpfte sich bei den

Skimeisterschaften 1940
des
Bannes und Untergaues Strohgäu

den **3.** Platz
im **Langlauf**

Der K.-Führer des Bannes 427

Leonberg, Februar 1940

. . . and two more good finishes.

Aside from swimming, skiing was a favorite sport of Erich Hartmann's. Here, making a bold jump over a wall.

The Korntal school ski team. From left, Erich, Wolfgang Schenk, Werner Schenk, Albert Maser, Otto Müller and brother Alfred Hartmann.

During this time, young love began with his future wife Usch, who was attending a school in the same area.

The first signs of requited love in the snow (And plans for the future were being forged).

Opposite: jumping a snow bank.

Military and Flight Training

Training at *Jagdfliegerschule* (fighter pilots' school) 2 in Zerbst/Anhalt.

1 Oct. 1940 - 28 Feb. 1941	Military basic training at Neukuhren/Ostpreussen
1 Mar. 1941 - 14 Oct. 1941	Flight training, *Kriegsschule* Berlin-Gatow
15 Oct. 1941 - 31 Jan. 1942	Pre-fighter school training in Lachen - Speyerdorf/ Pfalz
1 Feb. 1942 - 20 Aug. 1942	Fighter pilot school in Zerbst/Anhalt
21 Aug. 1942 - 10 Oct. 1942	*Jagdergänzungsgruppe Ost* in Gleiwitz/Oberschlesien

Neukuhren/Ostpreussen, a small town on the Baltic, was the place of induction and basic training for the armed forces.

The barracks of the *Fliegerausbildungs-regiment* (flight training regiment) 10 and the exercise grounds, called Sweat and Blood Field.''

Get up - lie down - shoot! The daily work quota of the recruits. Erich Hartmann, right.

The first photo of a proud *Fahnenjunkerflieger* Erich Hartmann in uniform in October 1940.

Hartmann's first trainer: Unteroffizier Gutt, here during sharpshooting training at 100 meters, unsupported prone position.

Erich Hartmann wrote to his girlfriend Ursula almost every day, who was now separated from him by over 1000 kilometers.

Posing for a photo album during a break in the ''fighting'' in the woods. Erich, top row, fourth from the left, leaning on two friends.

On 1 March 1941, Erich Hartmann had come to the *Luftkriegsschule 2* in Berlin-Gatow and received basic flight training there. The group photo show him in the middle among his course mates and flight instructors of *Aufsicht B*.

Fw 56 Stösser.

TRAINING AIRCRAFT

Bücker Bü 133
Jungmeister.

Go 145.

Junkers W 33.

Preparing for a flight in the Arado Ar 96.

Hartmann as a *Fähnrich* in pilot cap and boots at the *Jagdfliegervorschule* in Lachen-Speyerdorf in the spring of 1942.

The first captured Dutch Na 4 aircraft, of American make.

The Lachen-Speyerdorf airfield. In the background are the hangars, in the foreground a Bücker Bü 133 Jungmeister.

Erich Hartmann as an
Oberfähnrich, always ready for
a laugh.

Two close friends during the entire course of training. Left, "Bubi" Dose and "Bubi"
Hartmann in the early summer of 1942. Both were 20 years old at the time.

Oberfähnrich Hartmann during a
cram session of flight theory.

The desk of a *Jagdfliegeroberfähnrich*. Regulations, instructions, written work — and don't
forget pictures of the loved ones at home.

Daily flight duty and retraining on the Bf 109 E. All the fighter pilots awaiting their turn had to lie down at the take-off point and observe which mistakes their classmates made.

Changing students on an Arado Ar 96.

Fighter aircraft Fw 190 with the BMW twin-row radial engine.

The discontinued Arado Ar 68 fighter was still flown for type familiarization.

Hartmann before his first solo flight in a Messerschmitt Bf 109D. The flight instructor gives last-minute directions.

The instructor is always there.

On the earth once again. After a happy landing with the Bf 109.

The first students retrained on the Bf 109F. To the left stands Erich Hartmann, sitting in the light jacket is the flight instructor, and three fellow students.

Long cross-country flights were also part of the training program. Pre-flight preparation of a Junkers Ju 160 for a flight from Zerbst to Böblingen-Nürnberg-Zerbst.

In the cockpit during a flight from Zerbst to Böblingen. The flight went without a hitch.

After landing in Böblingen.

Between flights the pilots relaxed. Hartmann is third from right.

74

At home, cheerful Ursula was always waiting.

Happily reunited at home in Weil am Schönbuch for the first time after being apart for almost two years.

A happy couple on the balcony of Hartmann's family home.

DUTY ON THE EASTERN FRONT

Parked Bf 109 with iced wing and tail surfaces.

From Oct. 1942	with the 7th *Staffel*/JG 52
From May 1943	*Staffelführer* 7./JG 52
From Aug. 1943	*Staffelkapitän* 9./JG 52
From Oct. 1944	*Staffelführer* 7./JG 52 and deputy *Gruppenkommandeur*
From Dec. 1944	*Gruppenkommandeur* I/JG 53
From Feb. 1945	*Gruppenkommandeur* I/JG 52 until war's end

This is how new arrivals to the front would find their units.

Lt. Hartmann's first quarters. The tent was dug into the ground to give protection from shrapnel.

Soldatskaya in the Caucasus. Hartmann's first front-line airfield; upon being transferred to *Jagdgeschwader* 52, III *Gruppe*, 7 *Staffel*.

A Messerschmitt Bf 109G-4 is assigned to Lt. Hartmann, as is his first crew chief: Gefreiter Mertens. The aircraft is prepared for flight.

Winter is approaching, and one digs into the Russian earth.

Lt. Hartmann has reason to smile, as his winter construction is finished.

79

This is how it started: a shot-up J-16 Rata and a J-53.

A captured J-16 Rata, still camouflaged. The 12.7mm machine guns are clearly visible jutting out from the wings.

Friend and enemy peacefully united. A J-16 Rata and a Bf 109 G-4 in a size comparison.

Predecessor to the J-16 was the J-153, a bi-wing airplane (with somewhat less power that the J-16).

An even older U-2 model, the "*Rollbahn-Krähe*" (they were always flying at night).

A J-153 belly-landing — the trail of It grinding to a halt is visible under the fuselage. In the background is the U-2, the infamous "*Rollbahn-Krähe*", which flew nighttime harassment bombing missions.

The 7th *Staffel* presents itself. From right to left: Hfw. Friese, Olt. Betzüge, Staffeldienstoffizier, Ofw. Toll, Lt. Hartmann — the greenhorn, Hpt. Sommer, Staffelkapitän, Uffz. Dadd, Uffz. Hohenberg, Lt. Puls, Uffz. Heeg.

The *Staffel* duty room in a Russian peasant hut. In the background is a typical "Petchka", or oven. The whitewashed walls were painted by chief artist Ofw. Rossmann.

After four weeks on the front, Lt. Hartmann was sent to the field hospital at Jessentuki with jaundice, where he spent four weeks.

From time to time, the Krasnodar airfield was overcrowded with *Kampfgruppen*, Stukas, reconnaissance and fighter aircraft.

Even an Fw 200 "Condor" can break apart when overloaded on a hard landing.

In a high-spirited moment after his first air victory on 5 November 1942, Lt. Hartmann gives his weapons officer Rieger a ride on his shoulders.

A visit by *Geschwaderkommodore* Otl. Dieter Hrabak. In the center is a *Hauptfeldwebel* of the technical staff, on the left is a recipient of the Oak Leaves to the Knights' Cross, Lt. Zwernemann, whom the Kommodore is greeting.

The command post of the III Gruppe. In the middle is the command tent. to the right of that is the medical tent, left the ever-present radio intercept truck, listening to Russian radio traffic.

An Oak Leaf recipient, Lt. Alfred Grislawski, to the left and Lt. Hartmann to the right in front of the *Gruppe*'s command post at Fachsimpeln.

Uffz. Hohenberg and Lt. Hartmann during a stroll through Pyatigorsk, getting a quick bite to eat.

Poor weather keeps the fighters on the ground. Pyatigorsk, a typical district town in the Caucasus. Vehicles of the rear service units can be seen everywhere. The mountains hide deep inside the clouds.

Typical: catching forty winks between flights in a sparse peasant hut, which often served a dual role as quarters and command post.

After a murderous 800 kilometer retreat and large losses in materiel, all pilots of 7th *Staffel* had to go to Vienna to get new aircraft. A reception with the *Oberbürgermeister* Dr. Jung in the Vienna town hall was planned. From left to right: sitting, Dr. Jung, standing is a city councilman, Oak Leaves recipient Lt. Zwernemann, Knight's Cross wearer Ofw. Rossmann, Lt. Hartmann, Lt. Schüler.

After the reception, the obligatory souvenir photo. Lt. Hartmann is seventh from the right.

Back to the Eastern Front, to the Kuban bridgehead, the last hard fought-for bridgehead before the Crimea. One can see by this (humorous rendition of a travel advertisement) that the soldiers' sense of humor had not yet been defeated.

The command post of the III *Gruppe* on the Taman airfield at the Kuban bridgehead.

In front of the command post from left to right: Lt. Hartmann, Knight's Cross recipient Ofw. Rossmann, and Fw. Todd.

A typical fighter airfield. A circular landing area, around which the aircraft have been staggered and parked in such a way that any aircraft can be easily scrambled from its position. Here in Taman.

"Weisse 2" (White 2) shortly before takeoff. The pilot is in the cockpit, two mechanics taketurns winding the crank starter.

During daily inspection of a three-gun Bf 109G-7. Everything is prepared for an eventual scramble. The flaps are in take-off position. Trim set to zero, cockpit open, parachute in the seat, and seatbelts are laid to the outside and within reach to facilitate quick entry.

Between sorties the old hands talk with and advise the "greenhorns", with always close to the aircraft, ready for a scramble. Sitting from left to right with cap, Oak Leaves recipient Lt. Grislawski, above him Uffz. Hohenberg, behind him one of the technicians, standing is Knight's Cross recipient Dammers, sitting (white cap) is Knight's Cross recipient Rossmann, Lt. Hartmann with the scarf, next to him Lt. Puls.

In front of the "study" at Orel, Lt. Hartmann on the right with the cane. (When the weather was very warm, the typewriters were in the open).

In front of one of the most "feudal" quarters: Lt. Hartmann and "Spiess."

Last meeting with "Bubi" Dosen, left, who flew with the *Udet* Geschwader. Two days later, he was shot down.

The much longed for mail from home has finally made it through once more.

The *Staffel* mascot was a stray mongrel pup, which was spoiled by everyone.

In Ugrim near Byelgograd, shortly before the battle for Krakow and Kursk. The *Gruppe* was only seven miles from the front lines and had to camouflage itself like the army.

Hartmann's first *Gruppenkommandeur*, Major von Bonin, who fell in the summer of 1943.

Hartmann's second *Gruppenkommander* was Major Günther Rall.

The first air victories are shown on the rudder of his aircraft.

The ground crews of the *Staffel* knew no forty-hour weeks. They performed to such a degree in the near round-the-clock battle against mud, snow, heat and cold that it can hardly be described with words and pictures.

Lt. Hartmann and his wingman Ofw. Blesin talk with the tireless technical troops.

After eight months, the first return home on leave, during which he became engaged to Usch at Immenstadt on the Alpsee.

With Uncle Walter Denk in Immenstadt, after the engagement.

The Alpsee with the boathouses, one of which belongs to Hartmann's uncle.

Erich and his beloved
Usch.

Hartmann was called back early from leave to be named the commander of the 9th *Staffel*, III *Gruppe*, because his predecessor Lt. Korts had fallen in air combat while he was away.

The "Gelbe 1" (Yellow 1) of the *Karayastaffel*, a Bf 109 G-6, carried Hartmann from victory to victory.

Lt. Hartmann with his loyal crew chief, who he wanted to take with him to the *Karayastaffel* in the cockpit of his new "Gelbe 1", "Dicke Max" (Fat Max).

Lt. Hartmann in his first official car as *Staffelführer*.

Between deployments, Lt. Hartmann sits with his pilots during lunch (left, with cap).

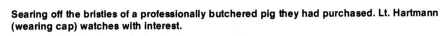

Searing off the bristles of a professionally butchered pig they had purchased. Lt. Hartmann (wearing cap) watches with interest.

From dogfight to dogfight. Despite all efforts, the retreat continues.

In front of a Finnish cabin in Dnepro, and they continued to go from place to place.

Finnish cabin in Apostlovo in slush and snow.

Unceasing frenzied movement between flying and fighting. Packing and unpacking. Here, Lt. Obleser and Lt. Perko wait for the uploading.

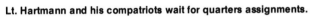

Lt. Hartmann and his compatriots wait for quarters assignments.

Loyal pilots of the *Karayastaffel* (left to right): Lt. Birkner, Uffz. Jünger, Lt. Puls, sitting on the left Lt. Blesin and Lt. Wester.

Between flying and moving, there were also inspections for lice. Hartmann on the left.

Suddenly, winter has arrived. Fueling and arming a Bf 109 in freezing cold.

**CHEF DER LUFTFLOTTE 4
UND BEFEHLSHABER SÜDOST**

Gefechtsstand, den 10.7.1943

Air victories came quickly. By October, Erich Hartmann had been awarded the Knight's Cross for his 75 victories.

Lt. Hartmann, III./J.G. 52

spreche ich zu seinem am 5.7.1943 erzielten 22. - 23.
Abschuß meine besondere Anerkennung aus.

I.V.

[signature]

General der Flieger.

After receiving the Knight's Cross, Lt. Hartmann was allowed to go on a fourteen-day leave. Even if the Do 23 was ancient, flying home on leave is always better than taking the train.

III/JAGDGESCHWADER R 52

Highpoints and Top Performances of the *Gruppe* from 1 December 1942 - 1 June 1944 (excerpts)

UGRIM, 3 July - 13 July 1943
In these few days the *Gruppe* achieved 117 air victories; on 4 July, Uffz. Meltzer's 25th victory was the 2500th of the *Gruppe*. Particularly successful on the 5 July were Fw. Toll with 5, Lt. Hartmann, Lt. Korts, Fw. Lohberg, Uffz. Meltzer, Uffz. Hohenberg, each with 4, OFw. Rossmann and Fw. Hauswirth each with 3 victories. On July 6, Lt. Wolf scored 3, on 7 July Lt. Hartmann scored 4, and on 8 July Hptm. Rall scored 4 air victories. On 6 July, Uffz. Meltzer scored his 34th and thereby the 800th of the 8th *Staffel*, and Lt. Hartmann's 22nd on 7 July was the 750th air victory of the 7th *Staffel*.

IVANOVKA, 20 July - 2 August 1943
On 28 July Hptm. Rall, and on 1 August Lt. Hartmann each scored 5 victories.

VARVAROVKA, 3 August - 5 August 1943
During these three days, the *Gruppe* was able to achieve 93 air victories, of which Lt. Hartmann alone scored 15, Lt. Korts 14, OFw. Steffen 9 and Lt. Puls 6 air victories. On 3 Aug, Lt. Korts destroyed his 75th, Lt. Hartmann, OFw. Steffen and Fw. Meltzer their 50th in air combat.

CHARKOV-ROGAN, 6 August - 12 August 1943
54 aircraft were shot down. On 7 August, Hptm. Rall scored his 175th air victory.

ODNYEPROPETROVSK, 9 September - 23 September 1943
Here, the *Gruppe* achieved 60 victories. Lt. Obleser scored his 50th on 18 September, and Lt. Hartmann his 100th on 20 September. September 19 was a day of celebration for the *Gruppe*, because the 8th and 9th *Staffels* achieved their 900th victories, and the *Gruppe* its 3000th.

NOVO SAPOROSHYE, 24 September - 15 October 1943
On 23 September, Hptm. Rall was received in the Führer's headquarters for the awarding of the Swords to the Oak Leaves with the Knight's Cross of the Iron Cross. From this location, the *Gruppe* was able to achieve 189 victories. The most successful pilots were: Lt. Bunsek with his 50th, Olt. Krupinski with his 125th, on 7 Oct. Lt. with his 75th, on 11 Oct., Lt. Hartmann with his 125th, on 12 Oct. Olt, Krupinski with his 150th air victory. The 7th *Staffel* was particularly successful here. On 1 Oct. it reported its 950th, and already by 13 Oct. it had its 1000th. On 10 Oct., Hptm Rall was the most successful pilot with his five victories.

APOSTOLOVO, 1 November 1943 - 6 January 1944
The commander of III/JG 52, Hptm Rall, was promoted to *Major* on 1 Nov 1943, and confirmed as commander. "It was a wild night of drinking." On 28 November, Major Rall became the second German fighter pilot to achieve 250 victories. Lt. Hartmann achieved his 150th on 13 December. Shortly before, he had been awarded the Knight's Cross.

NOVO KRASNOYE, 10 January - 22 February 1944

The most successful marksman this time was Lt. Hartmann, who on one occasion shot down 5 in one day, and on other 6.

KALINOVKA, 2 March, PRISKUROV, 3 March 1944

There were only a total of 15 air victories here, of which Lt. Hartmann alone shot down 10 enemy aircraft on one day, thereby achieving his 193rd - 202nd victories. On 3 Feb., Olt. Krupinski and Lt. Hartmann were each awarded the Oak Leaves to the Knight's Cross.

CRIMEA, SEVASTOPOL CHERSONES 10 April - 10 May

Despite the most difficult conditions and unclear situation, 93 air victories were achieved. The most successful were Lt. Hartmann and Fw. Birkner, both of whom achieved 21 air victories here, on several days shooting down more than three. On 5 May, Lt. Hartmann even shot down 6 enemy aircraft. On 23 April, Fw. Birkner shot down his 50th aircraft, and on 24 April the 8th *Staffel* reported its 1000th victory.

62

A peek at Erich Hartmann's flight logbook: from August 3-8 alone, 24 victories!

The first photo of Lt. Hartmann as a wearer of the Knight's Cross, which he was awarded on October 29, 1943 after 75 air victories.

During the address by the Burgermeister (Mayor). From left to right, the *Fliegerführer* Schumacher, Hartmann's father and mother, fiancee Usch and Lt. Hartmann.

Dieses Heldentum ist uns eine mahnende Verpflichtung!

Überaus herzlicher Empfang für Ritterkreuzträger Leutnant Erich Hartmann / Kreisleiter Oberbereichsleiter Siller beglückwünscht den jungen Fliegerhelden im Namen der Partei

—ied— Weil im Schönbuch, 17. Nov. 1943.

** Sehr zahlreich hat sich an diesem Abend die Bevölkerung von "Weil" vor dem Rathaus eingefunden, gilt es doch, dem Ritterkreuzträger Leutnant Erich Hartmann einen herzlichen Empfang zu bereiten. Die Jugend ist natürlich vollzählig erschienen. Dann kommt der junge Fliegerheld, begleitet von seinen Eltern und seiner hübschen Braut, und begibt sich durch das Spalier der glückstrahlenden Pimpfe ins festlich geschmückte Rathaus. Immer mehr Gäste finden sich ein. Mit Kreisleiter Oberbereichsleiter Siller ist Kreishauptamtsleiter Leik gekommen. Als Vertreter des Führers der NSFK.-Gruppe, Oberführer Kellner, ist der m. d. F. d. Standarte 101 beauftragte Obersturmführer Held anwesend. Weiter sieht man K.-Bannführer Koch und sonstige Vertreter der Partei und ihrer Gliederungen und der Wehrmacht. Im sinnvoll mit Fahnen und frischem Grün ausgestatteten Sitzungssaal erwarten den Kameraden von träger noch viele Freunde und die Flieger-HJ.

Zum Auftakt stimmt ein Schülerchor das Lied der Schule und der Flieger-HJ. an: "Deutschland, Deutschland, o heiliger Name..." und ein Sprechchor der HJ. kündet von der Kraft der Jugend. Ortsgruppenleiter Pg. Eberhardt spricht nach herzlichen Begrüßungsworten von der großen Freude und Glückwünschen von der Verleihung dieser hohen Tapferkeitsauszeichnung, die die Nachricht von der Auszeichnung durch den Führer an den "Sohn der Gemeinde" auslöste. Voll Bewunderung steht man vor der großen Leistung, höchstem Mut und dem fliegerischen Können. Die höchstem Mut und dem fliegerischen Können verkörpern. Dieses Heldentum ist uns eine mahnende Verpflichtung! Nach dem Lied "Heilig Vaterland" nimmt Bürgermeister Kärcher das Wort, um dem jungen Ritterkreuzträger den besonderen Stolz und die tiefe Dankbarkeit kundzutun, die die Gemeinde seinem Fliegerhelden gegenüber empfindet. Als äußeres Zeichen der Verbundenheit überreicht Pg. Kärcher dem Ritterkreuzträger

eine goldene Uhr und ein mit schönen Aufnahmen der Gemeinde Weil im Schönbuch ausgestattete Heimatmappe. Als der Raum erfüllt "Fliegerlied" anstimmt, ist der Raum erfüllt von der hinreißenden Kraft seiner Melodie. NSFK.-Obersturmführer Held überbringt zunächst die Grüße und Glückwünsche des verhinderten Gruppenführers und erinnerte dann an die Segelfliegerarbeit bei der Anfangs-gründe die Segelfliegerhelden die Anfangs-gründe auch unserem Fliegerhelden die Anfangs-gründe des Fliegens vermittelt hat. Der sehnlichste Wunsch aller jungen Segelflieger, einmal ein Fliegerheld zu werden, sei bei ihm in Erfüllung gegangen. Und nun bringt Kreisleiter Siller dem jungen Ritterkreuzträger zum Ausdruck seine herzlichsten Glückwünsche zum Heldentum, von dem stolzen Heldentum, das im deutschen Volke druck. Er spricht von dem stillen Heldentum, von die unsere tapfersten Kämpfer auszeichnet, von dem stolzen Heldentum, das im deutschen Volke tiefste Freude und Dankbarkeit auslöst. 148 Feindabschüsse habe der junge Ritterkreuzträger bereits erzielt. (Wir haben über die fliegerische Leistung des Fliegerhelden in der NS-Kreiszeitung bereits berichtet.) Das bedeutet fürwahr härtesten Einsatz an der vordersten Front. Als Erinnerungszeichen an den heutigen Ehrentag, der der Gemeinde Weil im Schönbuch zu einem Heldentag geworden ist, überreicht der Kreisleiter dem Ritterkreuzträger eine stattliche Statue "Der Athlet" als Symbol jugendlicher Kraft, gefertigt von der Künstlerhand von Hans Petzbach, Stuttgart.

Sichtlich bewegt dankt der junge Ritterkreuzträger für die ihm zuteil gewordene Ehrung. Er hätte seinen Dank nicht besser wie mit den soldatisch knappen Worten: "Ich habe nur meine Pflicht getan!" zum Ausdruck bringen können. Ein stilles Gedenken galt den toten Kameraden, die im Kampf für Deutschland, für ihre Heimat ihr Leben geopfert haben. Der Treuegruß an den Führer und die Lieder der Nation schließen die festliche Stunde, die ein stolzes Erinnerungsblatt in der Geschichte der Gemeinde Weil im Schönbuch einnehmen wird.

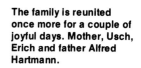

Newspaper article of Lt. Hartmann's return home to Weil im Schönbuch after being decorated with the Knight's Cross.

The family is reunited once more for a couple of joyful days. Mother, Usch, Erich and father Alfred Hartmann.

At the front once more. The action is harder and harder. It can hardly be said there is German air superiority.

But Lt. Hartmann's successes come faster and faster. He has already surpassed 100.

Again, new deployments are planned by the *Geschwaderstab* (headquarters). Lt. Hartmann's Kommodore (commander), Oberstlt. Dieter Hrabak (middle) bending over the map.

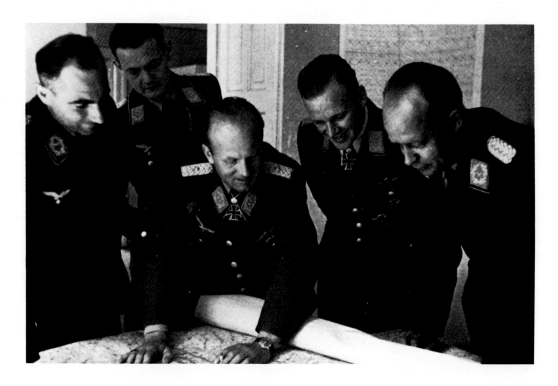

A little monkeying about in the snow.

Left from top to bottom:
Going home once more in March 1944 for the presentation of the Oak Leaves to the Knight's Cross after 202 air victories. A friendly Ju 88 crew is taking Lt. Hartmann, left, back to Germany.

Arrival and "the red carpet treatment" at the Sprottau airfield. In the middle, Lt. Hartmann, on the right the is air crew, to the left the airbase commander with his staff.

Hartmann (second from right) must talk about the front.

The awarding of the Oak Leaves by Adolf Hitler. From left: Maj. Wiese, Maj. Herget, Maj. Ademeit, an unidentified Hauptmann, Otl. Krupinski, Lt. Hartmann and an Oberfeldwebel of the anti-aircraft services.

The "Oak Leaves" are awarded.

Four fighter pilots of JG 52 at the reception at the *Führerhauptquartier* (Hitler's headquarters) in April 1944 on Obersalzberg mountain near Berchtesgaden. From left: Otl. Walter Krupinski, Maj. Gerhard Barkhorn, Maj. Johannes Wiese and Lt. Hartmann.

After the awards ceremony, and friendly exchange of experiences on the terrace of the mountain retreat. From left: Hartmann, Barkhorn and Wiese.

After wonderful days on leave, flying back to the front in a Bücker 181 from Böblingen.

Kommodore Oberstlt. Hrabak in the headquarters of the *Geschwader*.

Back on the front. Greetings in the command tent.

The *Staffel*'s little mascot "Struppi" gets its greetings, too.

110

The flight surgeon comes for routine altitude testing. Comrades watch amused as the oxygen is slowly deprived.

Olt. Hartmann is obviously happy with his high-altitude test results.

A *Grünherz-Geschwader* member again got off lightly.

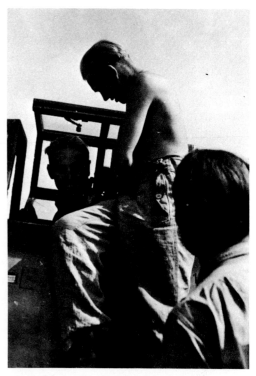

Olt. Hartmann is smiling — he has a new aircraft.

Ofw. Mertens helps his boss strap into the airplane.

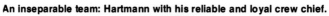

An inseparable team: Hartmann with his reliable and loyal crew chief.

Olt. Hartmann and his crew chief check replacement parts.

Posing for press photographers (this had to be done as well).

Even after the war, Hartmann's 1st crew chief was quite successful. Heinz Mertens with his wife and five of his children.

A visit and operations briefing by Kommodore Oberstlt. Hrabak (left). On the right: Olt. Hartmann, Lt. Gratz, Olt. Obleser and the *Kommandeur* of the III *Gruppe*, Hptm. Willi Batz.

The Kommodore Oberstlt. Dieter Hrabak (left) in conversation with Lt. Hartmann.

Hartmann helps his Kommodore Oberstlt. Hrabak strap in. Standing on the left are Olt. Obleser and Lt. Gratz.

The *Gruppenkommandeur* Hptm. Batz and his captains Olt. Obleser and Olt. Hartmann, left and right, are always ready to share a laugh.

Ein Württemberger unter den neuen Schwertträgern

dnb. Führerhauptquartier, 6. Juli.

Der Führer verlieh das Eichenlaub mit Schwertern zum Ritterkreuz des Eisernen Kreuzes an: Oberstleutnant Josef Priller, Kommodore eines Jagdgeschwaders, als 73., Major Friedrich Lang, Kommodore eines Schlachtgeschwaders, als 74. und Oberleutnant Erich Hartmann, Staffelkapitän in einem Jagdgeschwader, als 75. Soldaten der deutschen Wehrmacht.

Der 22jährige Oberleutnant Erich Hartmann steht mit 266 Luftsiegen in der vordersten Reihe der deutschen Jagdflieger. Als Sohn eines Arztes in Weißach (Kreis Leonberg, Württemberg) geboren, trat der Schüler der Nationalpolitischen Erziehungsanstalt im Herbst 1940 in die Luftwaffe ein.

Die Schwerter für Oblt. Erich Hartmann

** Wie wir bereits auf der 1. Seite unserer heutigen Ausgabe berichtet, wurde der inzwischen zum Oberleutnant beförderte Erich Hartmann, Staffelkapitän in einem Jagdgeschwader, vom Führer als 75. Soldaten der deutschen Wehrmacht nach 266 Luftsiegen mit dem Eichenlaub mit Schwertern zum Ritterkreuz des Eisernen Kreuzes ausgezeichnet. Mit stolzer Freude vernimmt gerade seine Heimatgemeinde Weil im Schönbuch diese Nachricht, ist doch einer der Unsrigen Träger dieser hohen Tapferkeitsauszeichnung. Er steht in der vordersten Reihe der deutschen Jagdflieger.

Schwerterträger mit 22 Jahren

Der schwäbische Oberleutnant Erich Hartmann unser erfolgreichster Jagdflieger

Von Kriegsberichter Ulrich Fiedler

rd. PK. Die Fliegerlaufbahn des schlanken, schneidigen württembergischen Oberleutnants Erich Hartmann, der mit mehr als 270 Luftsiegen der erfolgreichste deutsche Jäger an der Ostfront ist, hat erst im vierten Jahr dieses Krieges begonnen. Am 19. April 1922 als Sohn eines Arztes geboren und in Weil im Schönbuch beheimatet, verbrachte Oberleutnant Hartmann einige Jahre seiner Jugend mit seinen Eltern in Japan. Schon nach seiner Rückkehr stand es für den jungen HJ-Gefolgschaftsführer fest, daß er Flieger werden müsse. Der Drang dazu lag ihm wohl als Erbteil einer Mutter, einer bekannten Sportsfliegerin, im Blut. Am 1. Oktober 1940 trat Hartmann dann in die Luftwaffe ein. Genau zwei Jahre später kam er zu dem Südostraum beherrschenden Jagdgeschwader und Anfang Dezember 1942 konnte er seinen ersten Luftsieg erringen.

Als im Jahr 1943 die militärische Lage seine Jagdgruppe vom Kuban-Brückenkopf nach Norden auf das Festland führte, begann die eigentliche große Zeit des damaligen Leutnants. Bei dem Angriffsschlacht des Sommers bei Bjelgorod und den anschließenden Kämpfen im Raum Charkow fielen in kurzer Frist hintereinander 60 Feindmaschinen vor seinen Rohren. Bei den Abwehrbewegungen der deutschen Truppen über den Mius und den Dnjepr erzielte er in wenigen Wochen 75 weitere Luftsiege. Immer waren es vorwiegend Jagdflugzeuge, die Hartmann als Gegner suchte. Im Kurvenkampf überbot er keiner an Zähigkeit. Im Dahinjagen der schwirrenden Maschinen, in den entscheidenden Bruchteilen der für einen von beiden Gegnern letzten Sekunde spielte er die ganze verbissene Hartnäckigkeit aus, die ihm wohl neben dem Temperament in die Wiege gelegt hatte. Im Oktober 1943 wurde ihm das Ritterkreuz verliehen.

Wir trafen ihn bei dem Abschlußringen um die Krim wieder mit aufgekrempelten Ärmeln, die ihm am 4. März 1944 überreichte Eichenlaub im offenen Hemdausschnitt, die gekniffte Mütze schräg über die blonden Locken geschoben, so schlenderte er über den Flugplatz, ein frischer, unbekümmerter, durch nichts zu beeindruckender Flieger. Er kam herbei, um einen eben aus dem Wasser gezogenen sowjetischen Piloten in Empfang zu nehmen, den sein junger Katschmarek zur Strecke gebracht hatte. Hier zeigte sich eine weitere Fähigkeit des inzwischen zum Staffelkapitän aufgerückten Jagdfliegers: die Führung seiner weniger erfahrenen Kameraden. Wenn die Räder seiner startenden Me 109 ihre Rollfeld verlassen haben, wird Hartmann zum unerbittlichen Soldaten: gegen den Feind, gegen sich, gegen seiner Führung Anvertrauten.

Während der letzten Tage auf der Krim und bei den späteren Angriffskämpfen im Raum von Jassy stieg die Kurve des inzwischen mit der stellvertretenden Gruppenführung betrauten Zweiundzwanzigjährigen: innerhalb von 16 Einsatztagen waren es nicht weniger als 59 besiegte Feinde. Der Serienabschuß ist bezeichnend für das nun schon durch vielfache Erfahrungen gesteigerte Können des Oberleutnants. Sechsmal war das Tagesergebnis vom Luftsiege, fünfmal waren es sechs, zweimal sieben und einmal sogar zehn vom Himmel geholte Gegner. Fliegen und kämpfen, kämpfen und fliegen — am liebsten nun schon vom Morgengrauen bis zur Abenddämmerung, das ist die liebste Nervenspeise des bisher nahezu ungeschoren durch alle Erlebnisse höchster Gefahr gegangenen jungen Jagdfliegers. Einmal erwischte es ihn doch. Im Raum Bjelgorod—Charkow wurde er weit hinter den sowjetischen Linien abgeschossen. In zwei, die letzte Spannkraft von Geist und Körper abverlangenden Nächten schlug sich Hartmann zur eigenen Truppe durch.

Das Geschwader des Oberstleutnants Hrabak hat nach Oberstleutnant Graf, dem Stuttgarter Major Rall, Major Barkhorn und dem früh gefallenen Leutnant Stenbaß den fünften Schwerterträger in seinen Reihen zu verzeichnen. Männer dieses Schlages bestimmen den Geist, in dem die deutschen Jagdflieger unverdrossen und todesmutig den Kampf gegen eine zahlenmäßig überlegene Streitmacht an den gefährlichsten Punkten der Ostfront austragen.

Das ist unser Schwerterträger Oberleutnant Erich Hartmann

Von Kriegsberichter Richard Wolff

PK... im Osten.

Es ist ein junges, freies Gesicht unter einem nur mühsam gebändigten Haarschopf, das sich unter der sengenden Sonne des Ostens tief gebräunt hat. In diesem Gesicht stehen lebhaft und sprechend die blauen Augen, die mehr noch als der Mund etwas zu sagen scheinen, wenn um Luftschlachten und Abschüsse die Rede geht. Zwei Hände, die nur selten, dann aber um so lebhafter die Schilderung eines Erlebnisses durch eine leidenschaftliche knappe Bewegung unterstreichen, lassen in dieser ihrer bewußten Begrenzung nur wenig ahnen von dem unbändigen Schwung und dem draufgängerischen Schneid, die den Staffelkapitän Oberleutnant Erich Hartmann seit je geformt und zu einem Beispiel und Vorbild für seine Männer gemacht haben.

Blitzend und in der Sonne gleißend, liegt das Eichenlaub über dem dunklen Ritterkreuz. Das Lachen aber ist ein echt jungenhaftes, fröhliches Lachen, wie auch die Züge des erst 22-jährigen noch weich und gelöst sind, in dem aufgelockerten Sein der Ruhe zwischen den Einsätzen, in seiner lebendigen Freiheit und natürlichen Hingabe an diese Ruhe, wie an den Kampf und an die Dinge des Lebens! An ihrer Forderung und an ihren Gaben ist der junge Fliegeroffizier so recht das Abbild unserer deutschen Jugend, jener Jugend, deren Werden und Wachsen bestimmt wurde durch den kämpferischen Schwung einer Zeit, die unumstößliche Hingabe an den Sieg und an den festen Willen an Reich und Volk.

Aus der Einheit dieser Forderung und ihrer schon frühzeitig ausgeprägten soldatischen Haltung erwächst auch Wesen und Weg dieses jungen Jagdfliegers, dem der Führer am 4. März 1944 das Eichenlaub zum Ritterkreuz nach dem 202. Luftsieg verliehen hat, und der, wie wir bereits berichtet haben, nunmehr mit den Schwertern ausgezeichnet wurde. Der Weg aber, der zugleich das sinnfällige Ausdruck seines Wesens wird, hieß siegen und kämpfen, was als Grundsatz aller Flieger schlechthin zu gelten hat.

Wie immer in der Pause zwischen Ruhe und Luftkampf ist das Gesicht des Staffelkapitäns weich und warm. In den Mundwinkeln steht ein kaum verstecktes Lachen und die Hände halten ein Buch. Da läutet man „Alarm-Start". Schon springen die Flugzeugführer zu den Boxen der Jagdflugzeuge. Mit wenigen Schritten ist der Staffelkapitän an seiner Me 109. Mit einem federnden Sprung ist er in der Kabine, mit ruhigen und gelassenen Händen streift er die Fliegerkappe über. Sein Haar und das eine Wort „Alarm-Start" haben das junge Gesicht völlig verändert. Weniger als eine Sekunde hat genügt, aus diesem Gesicht alles Weiche fortzuwischen und seine Linien sind streng und hart geworden. Die seelische Bereitschaft zum Kampf und die Entschlossenheit zum Sieg drückt sich überraschend in ihnen aus, und die Augen, deren Blau plötzlich wie Stahl schimmert, wie dem Mund, der hart und seltsam geworden ist. Es ist nicht mehr das Gesicht eines 22-Jährigen, sondern eines Soldaten, eines Fliegers, der um die unerbittlichen Forderungen und Gesetze des Kampfes weiß, die er bisher mit jedem Einsatz meisterte und den Sieg mehr als 260 Mal zu sich zwang. Es ist das Gesicht des Kämpfers schlechthin, herb und spröde, aufgeschlossen und zugewandt dem Kommenden.

In der Ferne werden weit hinten die ersten heimkehrenden Me 109 sichtbar, werden größer und fallen schließlich wieder an den Feldflughafen ein. Als erster landet der Staffelkapitän und sein Rottenflieger. Wieder wie schon so oft hatte Oberleutnant Hartmann bereits die Gegner ausgemacht und seinen Kameraden durch die Bordverständigung den ungefähren Standort angegeben, als diese selbst noch nichts haben sehen können. Diese fast unglaubliche Schärfe der Augen, die jedem Flugzeugführer der Gruppe nur allzugut bekannt ist, hat viel in den Erfolgen des 22jährigen Jagdfliegers beigetragen, denn auf ihr gründet sich die Angriffsweise von Oberleutnant Hartmann. „Rangehen und abschießen" ist sein Wahlspruch. Und noch immer ist im Angriff überraschend gekommen, als die Bordwaffen des Gegners schnell waren und so konnte er eine bisher einmalige Leistung in der Geschichte des Luftkrieges in nur eineinhalb Jahren Fronteinsatz, der jüngste Ritter des Eisernen Kreuzes mit Eichenlaub und Schwertern der Luftwaffe, mehr als 260 einwandfrei erwiesene Luftsiege erringen.

Als er aus seinem Flugzeug springt, hat sich der helle Schweiß Bäche durch sein Gesicht gegraben, die Haare sind naß und verklebt. Die spannende Erregung steht noch um den Mund und in den Augen. Aber aus den federnden Schritten spricht die Spannkraft dieses Jagdfliegers und schon geht, als er sich flüchtig mit der Hand durch sein Haar fährt, ein Lächeln um seinen Mund, das zu einem befreiten Lachen wird, als einer seiner Männer eine Schilderung seines Kampfes gibt, den er eben herrlich bestanden hat. Und nun sind mit einem Mal die Züge wieder weich und aufgelockert. Es ist das alte, das schwunghafte Gesicht eines Offiziers, den der Krieg frühzeitig zum Kämpfer reifen ließ, der sich aber alles an Worten bewahrte, was ihm so recht Volk zugute kommen läßt.

Und ehe er wieder zum Buch greift, als sei er eben nicht erst von der schmalen Schwelle zurückgekommen, die zwischen Leben und Tod steht, nimmt er das Bild seiner jungen Braut zur Hand, und da steht wieder in seinen Zügen das helle unbekümmerte Leuchten einer reinen Jugend, die willig ihr Leben auf die große Opferschale des Krieges wirft, weil sie weiß, daß uns der Kampf das Recht zum Leben gibt.

The awarding of the "Swords" as reported in the press.

DER FÜHRER
UND OBERSTE BEFEHLSHABER
DER WEHRMACHT
HAT

DEM   Oberleutnant Erich H a r t m a n n

DAS

EICHENLAUB MIT SCHWERTERN
ZUM RITTERKREUZ
DES EISERNEN KREUZES

AM   2. Juli 1944   VERLIEHEN.

Hauptquartier d.Ob.d.L. . DEN 2O.Juli   1944

Der Chef des Luftwaffenpersonalamts

Generaloberst

And here he is once more. The awarding of the Swords on 24 July 1944 shortly after the assassination attempt on Hitler in the Wolf's Lair in Ostpreussen. Hitler can only offer his left hand. Second from left, Olt. Hartmann, after him the most successful night fighter pilot Wolfgang Schnaufer.

Hartmann and his wingman Uffz. Stumpf during an operations brief.

An aircraft is re-armed after returning from a sortie.

The bold and dangerous face of a Bf 109 of the "Gustav" series, with a powerful three-blade propeller, and a centrally firing 20mm cannon. Below the engine is the oil cooler, and behind the tires under the wings are the two radiators. To the right of the engine is the large air intake for the turbocharger.

Heave! - The men are always at work in full force.

Often in the mud, only human "horsepower" helps maintain operational readiness.

In the Spring and Fall came the feared periods of mud. Taxiing had to be done at a running pace with a technician on the wing so that the spraying mud did not stop up the radiator cooling fins.

Lucky again! A Bf 109 somersaulted in the mud.

A shot-down MiG-3 fighter. Description: 1200-1350hp, single seater, two machine guns, top speed 620-650km/h. Six RS 82 rockets could be mounted under each of the wings (Russian data). Actual performance was about 10% less.

A crash-landed Il-2 is examined with interest.

A Russian fighter SB-2 after an emergency landing. Description: Light fighter-bomber, two engines, each 960hp, 3-4 movable machine gun positions. Top speed at 5000 meters approximately 500 km/h, bombload 600-1000 kg, maximum range 2600 kilometers, service ceiling 8500m, production ceased in 1941.

Even a fighter pilot gets hungry once in a while.

The famous *Karayaherz* with the "Ursel" inscription on Hartmann's airplane.

For a diversion, the Krakau theatre troupe appeared once in a while and received hearty applause. In the first row from the left Olt. Obleser, Hartmann, flight surgeon Stefaner, the Kommodore Oberstlt. Hrabak and the Kommandeur Hptm. Willi Batz.

A last check of the engine and then its off to victory number 300.

OBERLEUTNANT HARTMANN'S 300th AIR VICTORY

Experienced through the radio communications: five victories in 12 minutes — few words for such a great feat.

The comrades left behind listen with great tension to the radio communications during the air combat of victory 300.

August 25, 1944

Shortly after lunch, Oberleutnant Hartmann took off on his first fighter sweep of the day. The ground radio station in operational. The radio-man sits in front of his log book, turning the knobs to fine tune his receiver, so that not even the slightest thing will go by.

Everyone was expecting victory number 300. Although there were still "10 Kilometers to go", in the jargon of the airmen, or 10 victories, but the atmosphere and the weather were such that it felt as though today would be the day on which the number one fighter pilot of the world would reach a victory total of 300.

The radio communications used by the pilots to converse with one another is extremely concise. Only the most important things are said, and then mostly using the briefest of words with specific meanings, which would often take the place of entire sentences. Sometimes there were very long pauses between individual conversations, sometimes the conversation was lighting quick with an almost dramatic escalation as one enemy aircraft fell after another in the course of a few minutes. Only a couple of words every now and then, and sometimes only one word would describe the action, but it was enough to keep those listening on the edge of their seats.

Oberleutnant Hartmann first reported at 1307 hours. Asking the ground station: Any reports of the enemy? — Affirmative. Enemy flight 50 kilometers south of S., course northwest — Thanks.

1309: Please continue reporting, we are approaching. 1313, to the other *Staffel*: Any contact with the enemy yet? No, not yet, were still approaching. 1314: Keep reporting!

Yes, number 300 has fallen.

1315: Ah, there they are - look out - shoot down!
1318: Heads up - shoot down! To Katschmarek: Go to the other side!
1322: Look out!
1325: Shoot down! Watch out beneath us and above!
1327: Shoot down! Watch your flying! Understood! - Impact!

Then it was quiet for a while. Only the crackling of static could be heard. A radio message to the *Staffel:* Oberleutnant Hartmann has five victories. To X: Oberleutnant Hartmann has five victories. To Y, to Z, everyone wants to know immediately. The excitement builds and snowballs. The opinions and estimates are now at 50:50. Up until now, the Oberleutnant's highest one-day total was ten. Will he do it? Will the unprecedented number of 300 be reached? All thoughts and every conversation revolves around this 300.

He is just 22 . . . someone says what everyone is thinking at the moment. He is only 22 and his all-conquering carefreeness of youth, his strongest and best attribute, is rewarded with the glowing culmination of a breathtaking course of victories won through the school of hard knocks. When he was sitting with us just an hour ago in front of the tent, it must have been that was feeling himself for a moment, reacting on feelings and not fully thinking.

Because he sat there, his shirt over his chest unbuttoned to the cool wind — we had just been talking about his fiancee, whose picture stood on the desk, and was gazing thoughtfully and pensively down at his chest, and suddenly broke out

in his youthful hearty laugh: "I'm getting a hair on my chest, I'm becoming a man!" At the same moment the alarm sounded, and the curtain fell on this small insight to which we were unexpectedly, and probably unknowingly, all witness. Everyone laughed at this statement full of self mockery, which, made in an off-handed way, combined his sense of tomfoolery and sense of insight into one. . .

1340: Shoot down. - he fell right out of the sky. - Impact fire on the street. - Break, break: over O, light fighter bombers and fighters. - Report from an aircraft: I'm over O, at 2000 meters. - Oberleutnant Hartmann 5 kilometers south of O. Air combat . . .

1343: Request: Any reports on of the enemy? . . . ah, back there . . . here come some more . . . 5km east of O, a new flight - an aircraft reports: My guns aren't firing. -

1345: Aircobras! . . . watch out above!

1350: Warning to Oberleutnant Hartmann: Look out! - Is that anti-aircraft firing? - Yes! Yes! Just before K. We're going lower.

1357: Land, I'll waggle my wings six times! (done as a celebration of victory, once for each aircraft downed)

Two hours later they took off again. Now everyone is gathered around the radioman and the miserable little headphones. It could happen at any moment. The radioman fine-tunes the receiver once more. He is a little nervous, afraid even, of missing the message of victory.

1544: Request to the ground station: Any reports of the enemy? None - Damn!, - why did they send us out!

Flowers are feverishly gathered and arranged.

125

The victory cane is quickly notched up to 300.

1550: Ground to Oberleutnant Hartmann: Enemy flight over S approaching.
1551: Eighth *Staffel* look out . . . Aircobras . . . crap.
1600: Shoot down —
1603: Shoot down —
1606: Look out to the rear and above! To the right of us, Aeras - Shoot down!
1607: Look out overhead! —
1609: He'll get his! - Look out! - Shoot down! Call from Katschmarek: Congratulations on number 300!
Call from the ground station: Congratulations!

For the next five minutes the radioman can receive no messages. Everything is going crazy, and he cannot understand a single word in the excitement and noise. Then it continued . . .
1615: Six kilometers west of S, light fighter-bombers, altitude 2000 - circling - Ah, new flight. They're P-2's!
1617: Eight kilometers east of O, altitude 3000, flight of bombers. - We won't make it there. Damn it. -
1619: Let's go!
1620: Shoot down - Impact explosion!
1623: To Oberleutnant Hartmann. Look out, behind to the left and below us are to aircraft, and one is a fighter.
1627: On our left a sole aircraft. - Ours.
1629: Watch out to the rear! - Understood. - Then a break.
1635: The *Geschwader* sends its congratulations!
1637: Land. I'll waggle five times!

And then the 22-year old Oberleutnant from Württemberg buzzed the airfield five times and wagged his wings at each pass.

For the first time in the history of warfare a fighter pilot has achieved 300 victories. Two years ago, he was a blank page. He had no victories, no decorations, and no name. In the morning, at the latest, his name would be on everyone's lips, Oberleutnant Hartmann, wearer of the of the Oak Leaves with Swords, *Staffelkapitän* of the 9th *Staffel* of the most successful fighter squadron in the world . . .

There even had to be home-made cakes.

The banquet is prepared.

Finally ''Gelbe 1'' appears in low-level flight and wags his wings for the 300th time.

He has done it. One can see the stress of the last 50 minutes on his face. Ten victories in one day is a superb performance.

127

The first one to his position, as always, is "Bimmel", the loyal crew chief. He jumps onto the wings to congratulate his boss.

Now all the well-wishers are there. A hastily prepared wreath is hung about the victor's neck.

But a swallow of champagne doesn't seem to taste very good. It could not be properly cooled due to a lack of ice.

After the initial carrying on has subsided, another photo is made for the press.

A press interview with war correspondent Kirchhoff (left).

129

The commanding General Seidemann comes to offer congratulations.

Luftflottenchef Generaloberst Dessloch also congratulates Hartmann.

Even two residents from Weil im Schönbuch, who coincidentally were building roads in the area with the Todt Organization, came as surprise well-wishers.

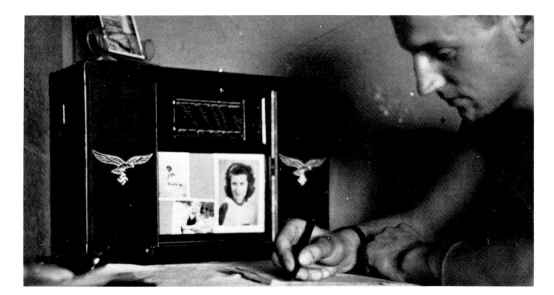

It is finally quiet once more and the daily letter to his fiancee is written.

Hartmann was not allowed to fly combat until the awarding of the "Diamonds." Now there is a lot of time for conversation.

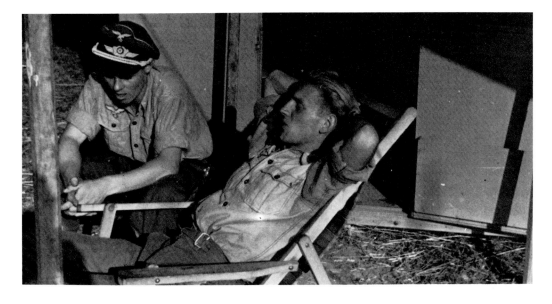

. . . and relaxation.

The teletype message from Adolf Hitler making Erich Hartmann the 18th member of the Wehrmacht to be decorated with Germany's highest honor.

Fernschreibstelle

Fernschreibname · Laufende Nr. · *409*

Angenommen
Aufgenommen

Datum: .... 19.....

um: .... Uhr

von: ....

durch: ....

Befördert:

Datum: .... 19.....

um: .... Uhr

an: ....

durch: ....

Rolle: ....

Vermerke:

Fernschreiben

```
++  Q E M    - FRR  WNOF   3701 25.8. 1900   =
AN HERRN OBERLEUTNANT ERICH HARTMANN, 9/ J. G . 52
WARZYN =
IN WUERDIGUNG IHRES IMMERWAEHRENDEN HELDENMUETIGEN EINSATZES
IM KAMPF FUER DIE FREIHEIT UNSERES VOLKES VERLEIHE ICH
IHNEN ANLAESZLICH IHRES 300 . LUFTSIEGES ALS 18. SOLDATEN
DER DEUTSCHEN WEHRMACHT DAS EICHENLAUB MIT SCHWERTERN UND
BRILLANTEN ZUM RITTERKREUZ DES EISERNEN KREUZES =
                      = A D O L F   H I T L E R    ++
```

The first and last time alone in the *Führer's* headquarters at the Wolf's Lair on August 25, 1944. The awarding of the "Oak Leaves with Swords and Diamonds."

26./8. 44.

VORLÄUFIGES BESITZZEUGNIS

DER FÜHRER
UND OBERSTE BEFEHLSHABER
DER WEHRMACHT
HAT

DEM Oberleutnant Erich Hartmann

DAS EICHENLAUB
MIT SCHWERTERN UND BRILLANTEN
ZUM RITTERKREUZ
DES EISERNEN KREUZES

AM   25. August 1944   VERLIEHEN.

Hauptquartier d.Ob.d.L., DEN 13. Oktober   1944
Der Chef der Personellen Rüstung und
Nationalsozialistischen Führung der Luftwaffe

Generaloberst

Lieber Hartmann!

[handwritten letter]

A last handshake and the decision to no longer be allowed to fly at the front. In the background is Hitler's Luftwaffe adjutant, Major von Below.

133

Fernſchreibſtelle

Fernſchreibname Laufende Nr.

0481

Angenommen
Aufgenommen
Datum: 28/8 19 44
um: 1/40 Uhr
von: Rad.
durch: T.

Befördert:
Datum: 19
um: Uhr
an:
durch:
Rolle:

Vermerke:

Fernſchreiben

```
+   SSD LBKW NR. 02516 28/8 1255 =
AN OBERLEUTNANT ERICH HARTMANN STAFFELKAPITAEN 9./J.G. 52 =
MEIN LIEBER HARTMANN,  MIT BEWUNDERUNG UND STOLZER FREUDE
BEGLUECKWUENSCHE ICH SIE ZU DER IHNEN VOM FUEHRER
VERLIEHENEN HOECHSTEN DEUTSCHEN TAPFERKEITSAUSZEICHNUNG.
IN EINEM SIEGESZUG OHNEGLEICHEN HABEN SIE DURCH
VORBILDLICHEN SCHNEID UND BEISPIELGEBENDE EINSATZFREUDIGKEIT
ALS ERSTER DEUTSCHER JAGDFLIEGER DIE EINZIGARTIGE ZAHL VON
301. ABSCHUESSEN ERREICHT.  IHRE IN DEN BESTEN TUGENDEN
UNVERGAENGLICHEN DEUTSCHEN FLIEGERGEISTES WURZELNDEN
LEISTUNGEN SCHREIBEN DER GESCHICHTE UNSERER LUFTWAFFE NEUE
RUHMREICHE SEITEN.  DAS DEUTSCHE VOLK ERBLICKT IN IHNEN
VOLL DANKBARKEIT EINEN SEINER KUEHNSTEN HELDEN.-
UNSERER JUGEND SIND SIE DURCH IHREN FANATISCHEN
KAMPFESWILLEN EIN LEUCHTENDES BEISPIEL UNBEZWINGBAREN
HELDENTUMS.  MIT MEINEN GRUESSEN UND MEINER ANERKENNUNG FUER
IHRE UEBERRAGENDEN ERFOLGE  VERBINDE ICH DEN WUNSCH, DASZ
IHNEN AUCH IN ZUKUNFT REICHES SOLDATENGLUECK BESCHIEDEN
SEIN MOEGE.=
IHR GOERING,  REICHSMARSCHALL DES GROSSDEUTSCHEN REICHES
UND OBERBEFEHLSHABER DER LUFTWAFFE.+
```

Unterſchrift des Aufgebers

Fernſprech-Anſchluß des Aufgebers

An additional congratulatory teletype message from the Commander-in-Chief of the Luftwaffe, Hermann Göring.

II/A

Vermerke: FL H Rttv Krakau / FSstelle: LIDR
Nr 1335

Fernschreiben

++++ SSD LJLM NR.1934 29.8. (2100).=

AN J. G. 52 . . = | An

- - - GLT D : - - AN GEN. KDO. ROEM. ACHT . FLG . KOR
- ROEM. ZWEI A .-om Aufgeber auszufüllen) | Bestimmungsort

AN J. G. 52 .-

AN ROEM. DREI ./ J. G. 52 . -

BEZUG : -- FS . LFL. KDO 6 / ROEM. ZWEI A 1 NR . 2245

V. 28.8.44. -

GEMAESS FS . OKL . LP 1 ROEM. EINS D NR . 41 555/44 V.

28.8.44 ERHAELT -- OBLT . (F) HARTMANN (ERICH), ROEM.

DREI ./ J. G. 52 , AB SOFORT FEINDSTARTVERBOT . OBLT.

HARTMANN WIRD MIT SOF . WIRKUNG IN DAS ERPROBUNGSKDO. 262

Ln. Nr. 36 011. 1100.   Unterschrift des Aufgebens   Fernspruch...

VERSETZT . MELDUNG BEI GEN. GALLAND , BERLIN - KLADOW .-

WIEDERHOLUNG AUF GRUND FERNSCHR . BESTAETIGUNG .=

LFL. KDO 6 , ROEM. ZWEI A 1 NR . 2283 +++

Notice of Hartmann's transfer to the Me 262 test unit near Berlin.

Back at *Karayastaffel*. Unfortunately, this time the good-bye is forever.

An Ilyushin bomber DB-3, a type which was used in the Spanish Civil War, after a forced landing. Description: Two engines, each with 1000hp. Crew of three, maximum speed at 6-7000 meters, 440 km/h. Bombload, 600 - 1000kg. No longer produced after 1941.

Russian bombers destroyed by low-level attack.

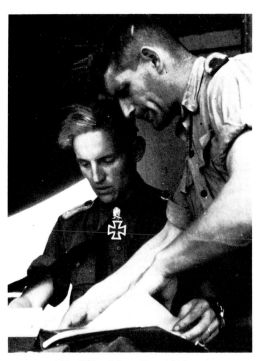

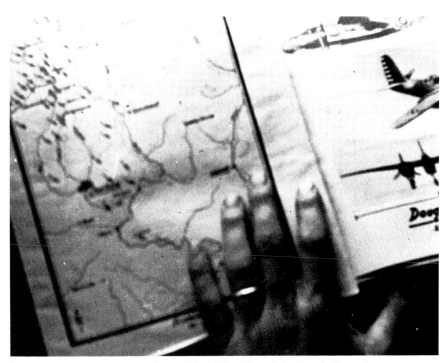

Uffz. Kalwelt from the orderly room presents Hartmann upon his departure from his *Karayastaffel* with a meticulously maintained war diary.

A look at Uffz. Kalwelt's precise war diary, with all the original combat reports, eye-witness reports (to Hartmann's dogfights), photographs of wingmen, maps indicating locations of dogfights, etc., which unfortunately Hartmann lost when he was turned over by the Americans to the Russians for imprisonment.

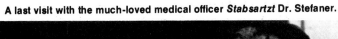

A last visit with the much-loved medical officer *Stabsartzt* Dr. Stefaner.

The loyal men of the *Karayastaffel* form up one more time for their commander.

Olt. Hartmann says good-bye with a handshake and thanks for the constant exemplary level of work performed. . .

. . . by each individual member of his team.

Heirats-Erlaubnisschein

Dem (Dienstgrad, Vor- und Zuname) **Oberleutnant (Tr.O.)**
Erich Hartmann

9./Jagdgeschwader 52

des (Truppenteil)

ist die Heirat mit (Vor- und Zuname) **Ursula Paetsch** (Ort und Kreis)

Tochter des zu **Stuttgart - Zuffenhausen** **Ingenieur Hermann Adolf Paetsch**

wohnhaften oder verstorbenen (Beruf, Vor- und Zuname) erlaubt worden.

Gef.Qu. den **26.August 1944**
Der Kommandierende General
des VIII.Fliegerkorps

(Ort)

(Unterschrift)

Generalleutnant.

(Dienstgrad, Dienststellung und Truppenteil)

Form. 53. Din A 5. Druckerei Gen.Kdo. V Stuttgart.

Despite the war, permission to be married still had to be obtained from the active officer corps of the old Luftwaffe.

Als Vermählte grüßen

Erich Hartmann
Oberleutnant

Frau Ursula
geb. Paetsch

Weil im Schönbuch

Bad Wiessee

9. September 1944

Then everything was ready. The wedding invitations were sent out.

139

Vacation at the *Jagdfliegerheim* (Fighter Pilots' Home) in Bad Wiessee at Tegernsee, where the pilots were rehabilitated for duty under the supervision of a doctor. Here, one did not feel the war, the care was excellent, and the spirits did not run out. The daily itinerary included exercise, walking, climbing, skiing, sailing and shooting clay pigeons.

The marriage took place on September 9, 1944. Traditionally, the bride is picked up at her place of residence. A bombing attack and horrendous traffic made the journey to the Bride quite an adventure.

The festivities have not yet begun. They have just been seated. The witnesses are Maj. Gerhard Barkhorn (left) and Hptm. Willi Batz (right).

The town hall and registry office of Bad Wiessee.

The faces are solemn and earnest. In the background, the school choir takes care of the musical arrangements.

The last words of the *Standesbeamter* (civil official presiding) echo through the room, then Erich and Usch are married.

The rings are exchanged. "Till death do us part."

In the meantime, all the fighter pilots from the *Jagdfliegerheim* have gathered to form a guard of honor in front of the town hall. Olt. Krupinski gives last-minute instructions.

The newly married couple emerges from the town hall, and the daggers are raised in honor.

A huge crowd has assembled to celebrate with the young couple.

The couple, flanked by both the witnesses Maj. Barkhorn and Hptm. Batz, is accompanied by the crowd to the *Jagdfliegerheim*.

The Certificate of Marriage.

Gültig zum Zwecke der Trauung

Standesamt Bad Wiessee   Familienbuch Nr. 16/41

Bescheinigung der Eheschließung

Zwischen dem Träger des Eichenlaubs mit Schwerter und Brillanten zum Ritterkreuz des Eisernen Kreuzes Oberleutnant Erich H a r t m a n n , evangelisch, wohnhaft in Weil im Schönbuch, Kreis Böblingen, derzeit im Felde,

und der Ursula Elisabeth Therese Auguste P a e t s c h , evangelisch,

wohnhaft in Stuttgart-Zuffenhausen, Unterländerstraße 72,

ist vor dem unterzeichneten Standesbeamten heute die Ehe geschlossen worden.

B a d W i e s s e e , den 10.September 1944

Der Standesbeamte:
In Vertretung:

Gebührenfrei.

Another photo memento of the bride and groom with the little bridesmaids and the many flowers presented by thrilled bystanders.

Friends and well-wishers hurry past. Here, Dr. Reichelt from Bad Wiessee.

Even the family dog "Struppi" was there.

After the hurly-burly wedding, a two-week honeymoon at Bad Wiessee. The couple enjoying the last of the fall sun at Tegernsee.

A visit with the marriage witness Gerhard Barkhorn, his wife Christel and little daughter.

A happy bunch during a walk in Bad Wiessee with Hptm. Frielinghaus (right) and Hptm. Krupinski (left).

During a visit with Göring, Hartmann asked for a lifting of the order forbidding him to fly in combat, which was granted after some hesitation.

Hartmann in a conversation with General Kastner before returning to the troops.

11 Männer
1676 Luftsiege

Ihr Geschwader erzielte insgesamt:

10 000 Abschüsse

**Oberleutnant Hartmann:
303 Luftsiege.**

Das As der Asse! Zum 300. Luftsieg die Brillanten! Erbe seines großen Vorgängers in der Führung der Staffel, des Brillantenträgers Oberstleutnants Graf. 22 Jahre alt. Saß 1940 noch auf der Schulbank. Sohn eines Arztes. Mutter eine bekannte Sportfliegerin. Geboren in Weissach bei Stuttgart.

**Major Barkhorn:
273 Luftsiege.**

Der erste Jäger mit tausend Feindeinsätzen. Nahschütze, Meister im Kurvenkampf. Aus der Flieger-HJ zur Luftwaffe. Gruppenkommandeur, Schwerterträger. 1920 in Königsberg als Sohn eines Stadtbauinspektors geboren. Erste Erfahrung 1940 gesammelt über London. Größte Erfolge gegen die Sowjets.

Hauptmann Batz: 208 Luftsiege.

Gruppenkommandeur. Sehr schnell in die vorderste Reihe der erfolgreichsten Flieger vorgekämpft. Große Erfolge im Kampf gegen zahlenmäßig weit überlegene Gegner und bei vielen Tiefangriffen. 1916 als Sohn eines städtischen Beamten in Bamberg geboren. Musikschüler, bevor er Soldat und Flieger wurde. Eichenlaubträger

**Oberleutnant Vönnekold:
134 Luftsiege.**

Staffelkapitän. Bei Verleihung des Ritterkreuzes Abschußziffer bereits über 100! Wegen Tapferkeit vor dem Feind zum Offizier befördert. Hamburger Kind, Sohn eines Hafenkontrolleurs. 24 Jahre alt. War früher Schlosser.

Leutnant Schall: 117 Luftsiege.

In kürzester Zeit Abschußziffer auf 117 geschraubt. Aus dem Wehrmachtbericht vom 1 September 1944: „Leutnant Schall, Flugzeugführer in einem Jagdgeschwader, schoß gestern 13 sowjetische Flugzeuge ab und erhöhte die Zahl seiner Luftsiege auf 106."

Leutnant Gratz: 116 Luftsiege.

Kam 1941 an den Südabschnitt der Ostfront. Februar 1942 erster Luftsieg. Juni der 54.! Ritterkreuz Juli 1942. Nach 83 Abschüssen nach dem Westen versetzt. Kühner Draufgänger, viele schneidig geflogene Tiefangriffe. Geboren 1919 zu Wiener-Neustadt.

Der Kommodore des Geschwaders: Oberstleutnant Hrabak.

Führer des erfolgreichsten deutschen Jagdgeschwaders. Eichenlaubträger. Hartnäckiger Kämpfer, hervorragender Organisator, Truppführer und Taktiker der Luftwaffe — mit einem Wort, eine Persönlichkeit. In Groß-Deuben 1914 als Sohn eines Baumeisters geboren. 126 Abschüsse.

**Hauptmann Borchers:
118 Luftsiege.**

Gruppenkommandeur, Ritterkreuzträger. Der glückliche Schütze des 10.000. Abschusses des Geschwaders. Einer der letzten aus den Tagen, da ein Mölders das ruhmreiche Geschwader führte. Geboren 1913 in Wendhausen. Vater Landwirt. Seine Frau: die Weltmeisterin im Skilauf Christl Cranz.

**Oberleutnant Obleser:
116 Luftsiege.**

Aus der Flieger-HJ. Begeisterter Segelflieger beim erster Feindflug im Osten auch der erste Abschuß. Zwei Monate später der 25. Gegner heruntergeholt. Ritterkreuzträger. Geboren 1923 in Pottenstein, Baden.

PK.-Aufnahmen: Kriegsberichter Dach.

Leutnant Birkner: 101 Luftsiege.

In achteinhalbmonatigem Einsatz 90 feindliche Flugzeuge vom östlichen Himmel heruntergeholt. War Rottenflieger von Major Rall, fliegt nun in der Staffel von Oberleutnant Hartmann, dem erfolgreichsten Jagdflieger. 23 Jahre alt. Sohn eines Oberstleutnants. Ritterkreuzträger.

**...und der Nachwuchs: Lt. R.:
64 Luftsiege.**

Vom gleichen glühenden Kampfgeist beseelt wie die „Alten", drängt der Nachwuchs nach vorn. Angehöriger der erfolgreichsten Jagdstaffel der Welt sein zu dürfen, ist für die jungen Flieger Ehre und Verpflichtung zugleich.

Hartmann meets with the old familiar faces on the front once more. Only the Kommodore of JG 52, Oberstlt. Dieter Hraak has been transferred to another *Geschwader*.

The weather is an enemy: either mud or..

... biting "Siberian" cold made the men and machines hard to deal with in the winter. A Bf 109 is prepared for take-off. In the foreground is the flashing light system used to scramble the *Rotte* or *Schwarm* on alert.

A Bf 109 ready for a winter take-off warming up its engine.

Ground crew members sit on the wings to guide the pilot along the narrow, frozen runway with hand signals, because his forward vision is obscured by the long nose of the engine.

The new Kommodore is Oberstlt. Hermann Graf, also a recipient of the "Diamonds", and well known from the battle of Stalingrad.

Hartmann assumed command of the 6th *Staffel* in the II *Gruppe*, commanded by one of the witnesses at his wedding, Maj. Barkhorn.

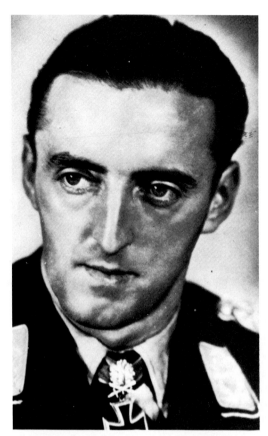 

Graf was not only a good pilot, but he could ride as well, as here in the area of Bucharest. He was also an enthusiastic soccer player, and at one time founded the red *Jäger*'s soccer team and was even its goalie.

Hptm. Hartmann at his new *Staffel*. "Bimmel" Mertens, who was also transferred to the 6th *Staffel*, has not arrived yet.

Landing prior to his first flight in unfamiliar surroundings and territory, but nothing has been forgotten.

Kommandeur Gerhard Barkhorn (left) and his adjutant Will van de Camp at a farewell party at the Hungarian *Staffel*.

The new *Gruppenführer* is Hptm. Hartmann, here with the Hungarian fighter pilot comrades under his command. On the right is Lazzi Bodjondi and the *Staffelkapitän* of the Hungarians.

Hptm. Hartmann and Lazzi Bodjondi became close friends.

Even in Hungary there were periods of mud in the fall.

On 1 November 1944, Hptm. Hartmann was named commander of the I *Gruppe* of JG 52. The *Gruppe* has fallen out for the change of command. In front is Hptm. Hartmann, next to him the old commander Maj. Adolf Borchers.

Kommodore Oberstlt. Hermann Graf (center) at the change of command ceremony.

The inspection of the unit ends the change of command; in the foreground in Oberstlt. Graf.

The new
Gruppenkommandeur
Hptm. Erich Hartmann.

Olt. Walter Wolfraum,
Staffelkapitän in
Hartmann's *Gruppe*.

During a visit with his *Staffel*. Center: Hptm. Müller with his pilots.

Visiting the 2nd and 3rd *Staffels*. Center: Hptm. Hartmann, left in the leather jacket is Olt. Wolfrum, *Staffelkapitän* of the 2nd, and right (without a hat) is Hptm. Trenkel.

Maj. Heinz "Prizel" Baer was Hartmann's commander and flight instructor during his retraining. He himself had 220 victories and 16 victories with the Me 262. Hw was a much-admired and outstanding pilot.

A temporary duty and retraining on the Me 262 at *Lager Lechfeld*, south of Augsburg. This is the new Me 262 with two jet engines.

In March 1945, Hartmann brought his young wife to the wife of his *Gruppe* adjutant van de Camp, Bobby van de Camp in Rottenbuch at Schongau/Obb.

Here, in the so-called Bräuhaus is where Usch Hartmann was at the end of the war and for the entry of the American forces. She hoped for a speedy reunion with her husband, but had to wait 10 1/2 years for that to come about. To the left, Bobby and Will van de Camp as wedding guests at the Hartmann's.

Hptm. Hartmann after his 350th aerial victory on April 17, 1945.

A friend to foe picture. Always come out of the sun, shoot at the closest range and disengage immediately.

The Oak Leaves with Swords and Diamonds to the Knight's Cross of the Iron Cross, up until shortly before the end of the Second World War the highest German decoration.

THE ODYSSEY

Miserable loneliness of the prison camp in the Siberian cold behind barbed wire.

Aug. 1945 - Oct. 1945	Moorlager Kirov
Oct. 1945 - Oct. 1947	KGF-camp, Gryazovets
Oct. 1947 - Oct. 1949	KGF-camp, Cherepovets
Oct. 1949 - Dec. 1949	KGF-camp, Ivanovka (1st trial)
Dec. 1949 - May 1950	GPU prison, Ivanovo
May 1950 - Nov. 1950	KZ camp Shachtu (2nd trial)
Nov. 1950 - May 1952	GPU camp Novotsherkaask
May 1952 - Nov. 1952	KZ camp Asbest
Nov. 1952 - Aug. 1954	KZ prison camp Degtyarka
Aug. 1954 - Oct. 1954	GPU prison Sverdlovsk
Oct. 1954 - Oct. 1955	GPU prison Novotsherkaask

The first photograph taken shortly after being handed over to the Russian by the Americans, taken at the Neubistritz reception camp in Czechoslovakia. Hartmann is sitting, and leaning on the table is Olt. Wolfrum.

Hartmann writes his first sign of life to his wife Usch, which was actually able to be smuggled out in June of 1945 by Olt. Wolfrum on a bicycle, who had been released from the camp due to a hip wound.

In ten years of imprisonment by the Russians, Hartmann was only able to send four pictures to his wife Usch as signs of life, all from camp 7150 in Gryasovets.

Forestry work in extreme cold. A picture which speaks for itself.

Camp 7150 in Gryasovets. Barracks for four hundred men. The prisoners lay in three tiers, the width of each plank bed was only 50cm.

Erich Hartmann in a little birch tree forest at the Gryasovets camp is happy about the arrival of a response card with a photo from his wife.

In July 1948 in the "Fliegerecke", or pilots' corner, which was a bench fashioned out of birch wood, where the pilots Maj. Bühligen, Daries, Assi Hahn, Ellerbrock and Maj. Ewald met every day.

Camp 7150 in Gryasovets, a collection camp, was probably the most humanely run camp in the Soviet Union. The camp commander was a Colonel Sirma. The camp street, above right are the prisoners' barracks, in the left foreground a wooden house of the *Antifa* and camp workers. In the foreground can be seen a bridge over a brook flowing through the camp. On the camp street are prisoners of war in winter clothing, cotton wool jackets and felt boots.

Assi Hahn with his *Gruppe*'s mascot before his imprisonment. Even then he had a leaning toward the sensational.

Maj. Hartmann's last photograph during his imprisonment in Russia, taken in November, 1948.

"Assi" Hans Hahn as he was during his heyday with 108 victories, fell into Russian hands by way of an emergency landing behind Russian lines in 1943. He was released at the end of 1949.

A typical interior barracks scene. Three-tiered plank beds for 200-400 men, according to the size of the barracks. All the furnishings were built by the men themselves.

A Russian KGF-postcard
with a response section.
Hartmann was not
allowed to send his first
card until six months after
his internment. He was
allowed 25 words.

Союз Обществ Красного Креста и Красного Полумесяца
СССР

Бесплатно
Franc de port

ПОЧТОВАЯ КАРТОЧКА
Carte postale

Кому (Destinataire) *Frau Ursula Hartmann*

Куда (Adresse) *Stuttgart - Züffenhausen 1/3 ald.*

(страна, город, улица, № дома, округ, село, деревня)

Unterländerstr. 72 USA zone

Отправитель (Expéditeur)

Фамилия и имя отправителя *Гартманн Эрих Альфред*
Nom de l'expéditeur

СССР Москва

Почтовый адрес отправителя *№1 51.10/52*
Adresse de l'expéditeur

Союз Обществ Красного Креста и Красного Полумесяца
СССР

Бесплатно
Franc de port

ПОЧТОВАЯ КАРТОЧКА
Carte postale

Кому (Destinataire) *Гартманн Эрих Альфред*

Куда (Adresse) *СССР Москва №1 51.10/52*

(страна, город, улица, № дома, округ, село, деревня)

Отправитель (Expéditeur)

Фамилия и имя
Nom de l'expéditeur

Почтовый адрес отправителя
Adresse de l'expéditeur

Prière d'écrire sur carte postale, autrement ces lettres ne seront pas remises au destinataire.

Lettre au verso.

The old stone house in the camp. It had been a prisoner of war camp in the First World War.

The camp orchestra under the direction of Hans Carste, which he had formed with considerable effort. Behind the orchestra is the political training barracks, called the Club, in which prisoners of war were to have been retrained to communism.

A view of the camp during the short summer, as seen from the laundry. Above right and left are the prisoners' barracks, occupied by 200-400 prisoners. Above center is the medical aid station, to the far left on the street is the housing for the camp workers. Just to the right of the wash stands one can see the brook which flowed through the camp. The "death zone", twin rows of barbed wire, can be seen in the upper right corner. To the extreme upper right is a watchtower.

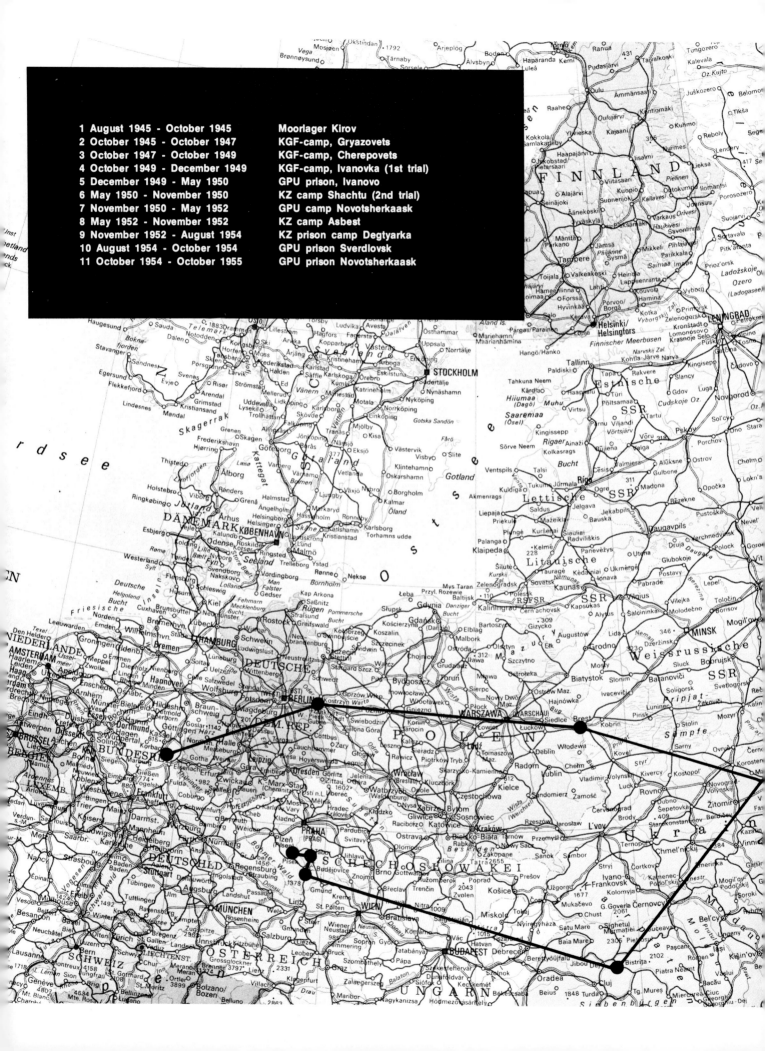

1 August 1945 - October 1945   Moorlager Kirov
2 October 1945 - October 1947   KGF-camp, Gryazovets
3 October 1947 - October 1949   KGF-camp, Cherepovets
4 October 1949 - December 1949   KGF-camp, Ivanovka (1st trial)
5 December 1949 - May 1950   GPU prison, Ivanovo
6 May 1950 - November 1950   KZ camp Shachtu (2nd trial)
7 November 1950 - May 1952   GPU camp Novotsherkaask
8 May 1952 - November 1952   KZ camp Asbest
9 November 1952 - August 1954   KZ prison camp Degtyarka
10 August 1954 - October 1954   GPU prison Sverdlovsk
11 October 1954 - October 1955   GPU prison Novotsherkaask

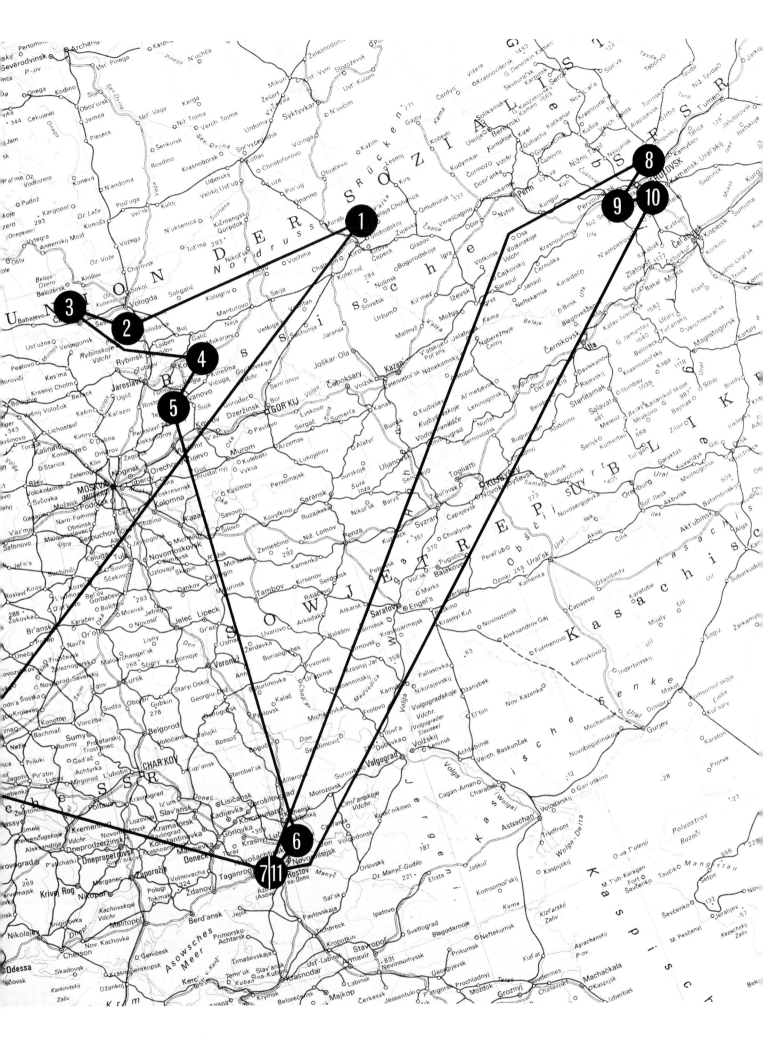

A poster of the SPD (a German political party) from forty years ago (depicting the Soviet Union as a prison for "hundreds of thousands of prisoners of war, civilian internees, people who helped the Wehrmacht, Red Cross nurses and women" in a plea for help).

Typical prison work on 600 grams of bread, 5 grams of fat, 20 grams of sugar, 2.75 liters of thin soup and a small ladle of oatmeal or thick maize porridge per day. For officers, there was an additional 15 *Papirossi* cigarettes while teams got 50 grams of *machorka* tobacco.

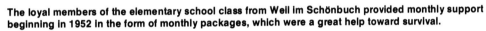

The loyal members of the elementary school class from Weil im Schönbuch provided monthly support beginning in 1952 in the form of monthly packages, which were a great help toward survival.

In the Soviet Union, a ridiculous shred of paper decides on life or death. This is the original 1949 document from the court sentencing Hartmann to 25 years forced labor.

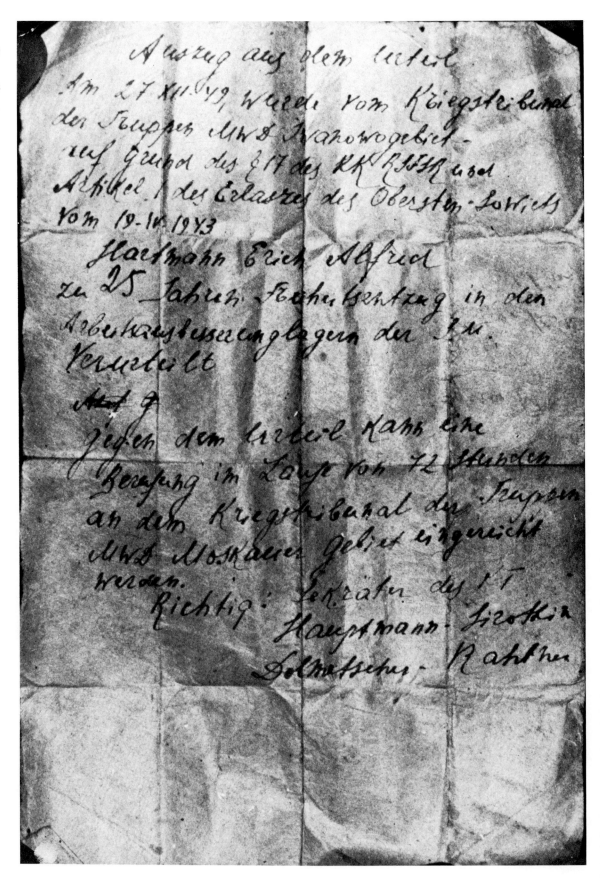

This is the way the normal life of the common masses looked in the Soviet Union.

The typical interior of a Soviet peasant house, one room where grandparents, parents and children all lived. The large clay oven served for heating as well as for cooking.

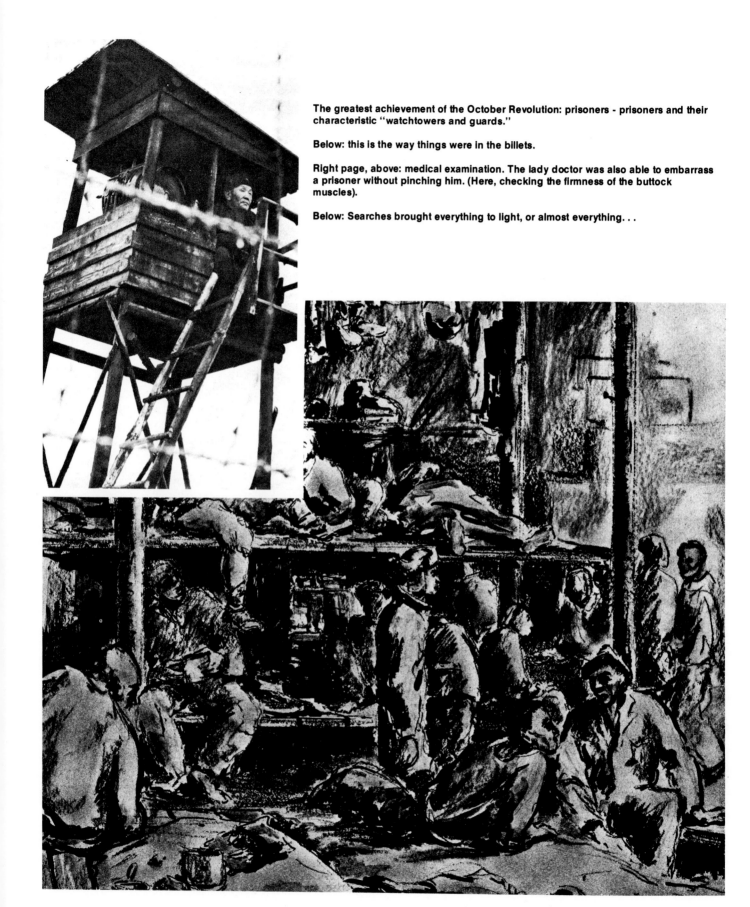

The greatest achievement of the October Revolution: prisoners - prisoners and their characteristic "watchtowers and guards."

Below: this is the way things were in the billets.

Right page, above: medical examination. The lady doctor was also able to embarrass a prisoner without pinching him. (Here, checking the firmness of the buttock muscles).

Below: Searches brought everything to light, or almost everything. . .

Hartmann's face after ten years in Soviet prisons and concentration camps speaks volumes. Photo taken at the Friedland camp during his return home.

During his official visit to Moscow, *Bundeskanzler* (Chancellor) Konrad Adenauer also secured Erich Hartmann's release from Soviet imprisonment.

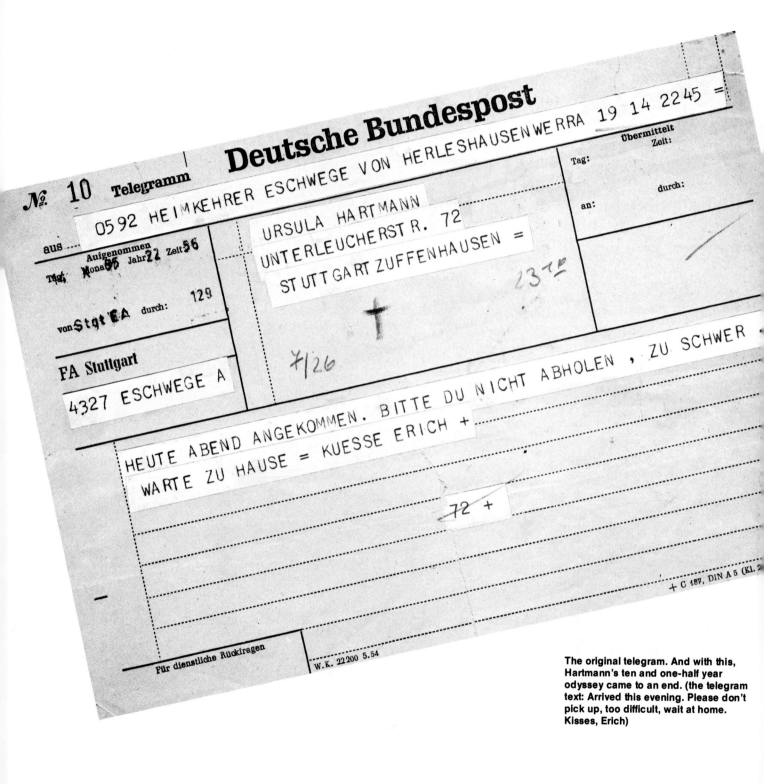

Deutsche Bundespost

№ 10 Telegramm

0592 HEIMKEHRER ESCHWEGE VON HERLESHAUSENWERRA 19 14 2245 =

aus

Aufgenommen
Tag: Monat Jahr 22 Zeit 56

von Stgt EA durch: 129

FA Stuttgart

4327 ESCHWEGE A

URSULA HARTMANN
UNTERLEUCHERSTR. 72
STUTTGART ZUFFENHAUSEN =

HEUTE ABEND ANGEKOMMEN. BITTE DU NICHT ABHOLEN , ZU SCHWER

WARTE ZU HAUSE = KUESSE ERICH +

72 +

Übermittelt
Zeit:

Tag:

an:

durch:

+ C 187, DIN A 5 (Kl.

Für dienstliche Rückfragen

W.K. 22200 5.54

The original telegram. And with this, Hartmann's ten and one-half year odyssey came to an end. (the telegram text: Arrived this evening. Please don't pick up, too difficult, wait at home. Kisses, Erich)

Greeted upon his return in Friedland by a former fellow sufferer.

The first telegram from Herleshausen to his wife Usch.

. . . finally free!

The first flowers in freedom.

Getting outfitted in Friedland. Trying on new shoes.

Trying on the first, new civilian jacket. What a feeling that was!

Assi Hahn, who was released from Soviet imprisonment in 1949, appears in Friedland to greet Hartmann.

Oberst Herzog speaks in freedom for the first time for all those whose returned home late.

Hartmann's arrival in his hometown of Weil im Schönbuch on October 17, 1955.

Hartmann greets his mother in front of his parents' house. His father had died in 1952.

Even his old classmates
were there to greet him
and celebrate his return.

The *Bürgermeister*
(major) waits for
Hartmann in front of his
home with flowers.

After ten and one half long years finally home again with Usch, who had waited for him unwaveringly.
And the reporters are there already.

A cheerful welcome home toast with brother Alfred (left).

SPEECH BEFORE HIS HOMETOWN
after returning from Russian imprisonment (excerpts)

I would first like to give my heartfelt thanks for this reception my town has prepared for me yesterday and today. I know, I can hardly find the words to express the feelings in the heart of an old soldier when, after ten years of slavery, ten years of experiencing cruelty, suppression and no rights, he can suddenly see that he has not lost his human face, but rather that he can once again be a man among men. And this in the region where he grew up, where he feels at home, where he has his friends, his wife and his family around him, my Weil, where I have always felt, and in the future always will feel, the most at home. That I could return to this Weil with these wonderful people! It is terribly hard to be able to thank you for all that, and to say it to you in words. At the moment, I can only say: Thank you very, very much!

It was the sole support from the military members, the town, my schoolmates, which continuously gave me the strength to get through.

I can only say to all the townspeople of Weil who are still waiting for their military men and do not know what has happened to them: I cannot raise your hopes, but I also cannot say that there is no hope. The matter with Russia is not over with. I believe that the best thing to do tonight is to take you back to the year 1950, to the year when the life of suffering began for all the German soldiers.

I begin with this, so that you may see, how the sentencing proceeded, so that you may see that all those people who were held back were not sentenced because they had committed some crime or offense, but rather out of cold sober calculation. They wanted make a profit from us in the future, a completely typical human profit.

... the trial took place in a small room in the camp headquarters. Sitting there were a Russian captain, flanked by a fantastically dressed-up woman, a young lieutenant, and a man and a woman acting as interpreters. Behind them along the wall stood about 5-6 guarding soldiers under arms.

As I came into the room, it was revealed to me that this was a military tribunal, and that I had to answer to charges before this court of being an accessory to war crimes according to (law) 17/1. I still had not taken the whole thing seriously. But the affair became quite serious when this man read out something in Russian. It became rather clear that the law 17/1 could only be applied to citizens of Russian, but was being applied to all foreigners after the war.

The entire process lasted about ten minutes. I was accused of:
• the shooting down of many aircraft - a pure war-time matter, this was. It was either him or me,-
• Point 2: that I had shot and killed 780 civilians in a village.

In response to my point that I was never in this area and that a pilot does not have the time to do such things, that he could only do one thing or the other, I was told: Yes, yes, we know that but it doesn't matter. My response to that was: "Yes, then the number is too high for me, because you surely know that we only had 120 rounds of ammunition." "Doesn't matter, every bullet hit 3 or 4 people."
• Point 3 charged me with having shot up a flour mill, which previously had produced 16 tons of flour a day, and afterwards only produced one ton.

With that the trial was over. There was still a personal interview, but I declined this. I was given a small scrap of paper with the attestation of the 25-year sentence, which I had received there at the window.

The next day there were about 80-100 Russian soldiers placed around the square and we had to take our first steps into imprisonment. Everything which reminded us of home, all the letters, photographs, whatever mementos which were still there were taken away from us. We were allowed to keep one pair of dungaree pants, one dungaree jacket and one cotton wool jacket, everything else was disposed of. When I asked a Russian officer if I could at least be allowed to

keep a picture of my wife, he answered "It not necessary, she has Americans there, and can keep herself amused."

Then we went to the Gorki prison, where we were housed 40-50 men in one small room, without a barber and hardly any medical care. That was the most cruel time I experienced in my imprisonment. After complaints, demands and hunger-strikes, a Major came from Moscow on April 5th and explained to us that we were free once more and would fall under the old prisoner of war regulations. The care improved. Once again we received the so-called prisoner of war sentence. We got cigarettes and tobacco once more, and the whole regime was easier for us, so that we lived more normally in the prison.

When we asked if we could at least write letters again, we were told: "There's no need, in 2-3 weeks you can tell everything verbally."

On the eighth of May we were all loaded up, surrounded by searchlights, barbed wire, dogs and guards. When we asked if this was a transport to Germany, they said no, you can't be sent back to Germany at the moment, you have to spend two months in the south at a convalescent camp. You can't go back to Germany in this condition.

When we arrived at the Shertern camp on the Donetsbecken we were told: You are criminals and will be handled as such. Here there is work, work and more work and nothing else. If you work well, you will live longer. You can earn money. Work poorly and you'll die here.

The slavery started on the very first day. The entire camp immediately initiated a hunger strike. It was not as if one could even get used to the camp for a couple of days, rather one simply arrived and was immediately put to work. The work was like this: the people were led to the work site with dogs. The work area was cordoned off with barbed wire and the people were counted as they entered. Then they worked for 8-9 hours with a lunch break of 1/2 an hour to an hour, then it was back to the camp, ate, and collapsed, exhausted, slept, and the next day it started all over again. That is how it was all those years. . .

Our release came quite suddenly. On October 9th, suddenly four men at a time were taken to the attic of the prison, where the baggage was handed out to us. The next day we were taken to Rostow on a truck. There, they had a typical Russian send-off. On that morning, a Russian General came and conducted, or wanted to conduct, one more political speech. Apparently he thought that in their hour of going home, the Germans would be soft again. . .

Erich Hartmann speaks to his townspeople.

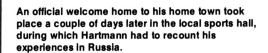

An official welcome home to his home town took place a couple of days later in the local sports hall, during which Hartmann had to recount his experiences in Russia.

HOME AGAIN -
BUT WHAT NOW?

Erich Hartmann was 33 years old. He even had his *Abiturzeugnis* (university entrance exam). But it was too late to study medicine.

Hartmann, on the left, Usch driving the tractor helping during the harvest. On the trailer is Christian Ulmer.

The reunited Hartmann's fully enjoying freedom and visiting old friends with their small car.

The Blühnbach castle in Austria. A visit to Hartmann's long-time friend from his imprisonment Harald von Bohlen und Halbach.

Harald von Bohlen und Halbach and Erich Hartmann swap experiences during a stroll.

The first meeting with his former *Gruppenadjutant* after 11 years. From left: Will vande Camp, Usch Hartmann, Bobby van de Camp and Erich Hartmann.

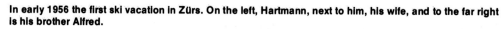

In early 1956 the first ski vacation in Zürs. On the left, Hartmann, next to him, his wife, and to the far right is his brother Alfred.

Hartmann learning the Christinia skiing technique.

Hartmann runs into his prisoner of war friend Dr. Eilmann (left). Next to Erich Hartmann is a girlfriend of his brother's and his brother Alfred.

A side trip to the Bodensee on the way home and, for the first time since their wedding, a meeting with the former flight surgeon from the *Jagdfliegerheim* in Bad Wiessee, Dr. Alfred Rossbach.

Their first summer
vacation together on the
North Sea, on the Island
of Sylt.

The unobstructed view
across the North Sea is
stunning.

Hartmann in the rear seat with "Prizel" Baer, Hartmann's commander during retraining on the Me 262, preparing to take off on a glider flight.

Hartmann is flying once more, but slower aircraft. His flight instructor Fritz König from the BWLV in Echterdingen.

Kirschenlohr, the loyal technician of the BWLV-school, starting the engine.

A licensed private pilot once again. Despite an 11-year reprieve, Hartmann has not forgotten how to fly.

The first meeting and exchange of ideas about a book in the summer of 1956. from left: Maj. a.D. (retired) "Prizel" Baer, USAF Colonel Ray Toliver, the later co-author of the book "Holt Hartmann vom Himmel", Erich Hartmann and Maj. Piepel at the Echterdingen airfield.

Further talks about a book took place at the Hartmann's in Weil im Schönbuch. To the left is an interpreter, Colonel Toliver, Usch and Erich Hartmann.

A daughter, Ursula-Isabel, was born to the Hartmann's on 23 February 1957. Mother beams. . .

. . . and father is also overjoyed.

Hartmann (arrow) in Landsberg during a "refresher course" conducted by the Americans.

THE BUNDESWEHR

A new drill begins in American markings and under American direction on a T-6, a two-seat trainer aircraft.

Hartmann's flight instructor: in the cockpit Capt. James Mungam, a real Texan.

The first course is completed, and his English is getting better day by day.

Flight instructor and student have become friends. The Mungams on the left and the Hartmann's in Garmisch over a farewell drink.

The Hartmann's en route from Landsberg to Fürstenfeldbruck. The fact that Hartmann also liked to go fast on the ground is betrayed by his means of transport.

Several former members of JG 52 meet again at Fürstenfeldbruck. From left to right, Maj. Barkhorn, Maj. Hartmann, Oberst Steinhoff and Maj. Rall, summer, 1957.

Final jet training flight from Fürstenfeldbruck to Ota near Lisbon, Portugal. Hartmann standing second from right.

The final portion of the flight training, gunnery training, took place in the United States, in Arizona, near the state capitol of Phoenix. Here in an aerial photo.

Participants from the left (standing): Otl. Barth, Maj. Dahlmann, Hptm. Schauder, Otl. Tettero, Maj. Hartmann, Hptm. Wegener, Maj. Grewe, Hptm. (unknown), Otl. Rall, sitting from left: Hptm. Obleser, Maj. Grasemann, Hptm. Lauxmann, Hptm. Bernhard, Hptm. von Berg, and standing is Otl. Proll.

Possible loads for the F-84 fighter-bomber.

The Germans in formation flight high above Arizona.

An F-84 fighter-bomber *Rotte* conducting bombing training in the Arizona desert.

Phoenix, Arizona in November of 1957: a cool drink and a swimming pool between duties. From left: Hptm. von Berg, Maj. Hartmann, Otl. Barth and the hostess Wylene Buzze.

Hartmann's best friends in America and hosts to Usch and Erich Hartmann: Wylene and Frank Buzze with Usch.

Discussing operations. From left, a USAF Captain, Otl. Proll an Maj. Hartmann.

Training successfully completed. Standing in front of an F-84 are, from left: Hptm. Obleser, Otl. Rall, Hptm. Schauder, Hptm. Wegener, Maj. Hartmann, Hptm. Bernhard and Olt. Tettero.

Presentation of the training certificate to Maj. Hartmann by the American training commander.

Final days in the USA and a good-bye to the most successful U.S. fighter of WWII, the P-51 Mustang. From left: Maj. Hartmann, Otl. Rall and Otl. Barth.

FIGHTER PILOT ONCE MORE

The aircraft markings are reminiscent of times past.

The final training took place at *Waffenschule* (Weapons School) 10 under the direction of Canadian flight instructors. Maj. Hartmann with the chief Canadian instructor Duke Warren.

A short operational discussion, and then off they go. Duke Warren left, Hartmann right.

One more 6-week course at the *Schule für Innere Führung der Bundeswehr* (a military leadership school) in Koblenz-Pfaffendorf. The soldier of the old style becomes a "civilian in uniform."

The course participants in an international group. British, Norwegian, French, Belgian, all countries are represented here.

January 1959, Ahlhorn in Oldenburg. The sleeping village, seen here from a bird's eye view, became Major Hartmann's first post-war domain. He built-up the first post-war German *Jagdgeschwader* at the airfield here.

The first self-designed unit crest of *Jagdgeschwader* 71. From bottom to top: black, red, golden sun, the NATO star in the sun's rays, and two flying swords, symbolizing the basic element of a fighter formation, the *Rotte*, above which is the new German pilots' badge.

Opposite:
The Ja 111, Kommodore Maj. Hartmann's aircraft. The marking of individual aircraft came about after many of the townsfolk complained of the noise after German aircraft suddenly appeared in the area again. In the event of any noise violations, the perpetrators were to be recognizable.

A formation of Canadair Sabre VI's of *Jagdgeschwader* 71 during operational training.

During the building-up of his *Geschwader*, Hartmann flew almost daily with his young pilots in order to teach them the art and tricks of combat flying.

The first flights of *Jagdgeschwader* 71 were controlled from this provisional tower.

A Sabre VI on approach to landing. One can clearly see the extended landing gear and deployed air brakes in the center of the fuselage.

Left: The instrument panel in front of the pilot. Above right: the forward portion of the left side service panel with throttle. Below: the right side service panel. A single pilot must be able to master all this in his sleep if he does not want to be a danger to himself or others.

The fighters had to be maintained every day by the ground crews.

Hartmann in the center, standing among his first young fighter pilots.

218

Uffz. Rack (without hat) accepts an aircraft from the chief mechanic.

One discussion with the *Geschwader* followed another, every day, because there were few precedents.

The three operational phases.

Maj. Hartmann accepts an aircraft from the technicians.

Preparation for take-off. Helmet and mask are already on, and now he must strap into the ejection seat.

The flight has ended. Mask off, canopy open and relax.

The first control room of the newly formed *Geschwader*. Orders, directives, and recommendations were drawn up at the green table. Kommodore Hartmann in the leather jacket, to the left the staff operations officer Hptm. Harms, the technical officer Maj. Kaiser, Staffelkapitän of the first *Staffel*, Hptm. Schmieder, Staffelkapitän of the second *Staffel*, Hptm. Drube, the flight surgeon Oberstabsartzt Dr. von Wardenburg and the NATO tactical advisor Capitän Willem Jansen of the Royal Dutch Air Force.

The big day has arrived — the of the activation of the first German *Jagdgeschwader* in June of 1959. The aircraft of the staff are lined up in front of the German and NATO flags.

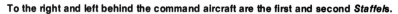

To the right and left behind the command aircraft are the first and second *Staffel*s.

The *Geschwader* forms up, flanked on the left by visitors.

The *Geschwader* with the music platoon and aircraft are formed to report.

Kommodore Maj. Hartmann shortly before reporting to the Inspekteur der Luftwaffe (Inspector General of the Luftwaffe).

Shortly after reporting to *Inspekteur General* Josef Kammhuber (above, center).

Inspekteur Generalleutnant Kammhuber during his address.

Honored guests.

Ceremonial inspection of the ranks: from the left Maj. Hartmann, Generalmajor Harlinghausen and Generalleutnant Kammhuber eye-to-eye with the men of the *Geschwader*.

Preparation for the *Geschwader*'s first flight presentation. The pilots climb aboard.

The *Geschwader* aircraft taxi closely behind one another for a simultaneous take-off in formation.

Inspekteur GenLt. Kammhuber and Kommodore Maj. Hartmann watch the first training achievements of the young pilots with interest.

The first overflight is in blocks of four aircraft.

The second overflight as three *Schwarm*s, in the lead is the staff *Schwarm*, on the left the 1st *Staffelschwarm*, on the right the 2nd *Staffelschwarm*.

On the third overflight, *Jagdgeschwader* 71 "paints" its number on the sky over Oldenburger Land.

Jagdgeschwader 71 in Dienst gestellt

Zahlreiche Ehrengäste und Zuschauer auf dem Flugplatz Ahlhorn

Ahlhorn — In einem feierlichen Akt stellte Sonnabendvormittag der Inspekteur der Luftwaffe, Generalleutnant Kammhuber, im Auftrage des verhinderten Bundesverteidigungsministers Franz-Josef Strauß das erste Nachkriegs-Jagdgeschwader der deutschen Luftwaffe auf seinem Heimatflugplatz Ahlhorn in Dienst. Nach altem fliegerischem Brauch gab Generalleutnant Kammhuber dem Jagdgeschwader, das den Namen JG 71 trägt und dessen Kommodore der aus dem Kriege bekannte Jagdflieger Erich Hartmann ist, „Hals und Beinbruch" und „Glück ab".

Zahlreiche Ehrengäste hatten sich eingefunden. Dazu Vertreter der anderen Luftwaffenverbände, des Heeres und der Marine, Vertreter der verschiedensten Behörden und Dienststellen und weite Kreise der Bevölkerung aus Ahlhorn und Umgebung. Von eigens errichteten Tribünen konnten alle das Geschehen und die durch Lautsprecher übertragenen Ansprachen gut verfolgen.

In einer Flugzeughalle war die Tribüne für die Ehrengäste aufgeschlagen. Die Rednertribüne war mit der schwarz-rot-goldenen Flagge der Bundesrepublik drapiert und von zwei Feldjägern in Marine-Uniform flankiert. Dahinter die Flaggen aller NATO-Mitgliedstaaten. Kurz nach 11 Uhr meldete Major Hartmann dem Inspekteur der Luftwaffe die mit Front zur Halle angetretene Ehrenkompanie mit einem Luftwaffen-Musikkorps aus Münster und das Geschwader. Zusammen mit General Harlinghausen, dem Kommandanten des Luftwaffenabschnittes Nord, schritt General Kammhuber die Front ab und besichtigte die dahinter abgestellten Maschinen.

In seiner Ansprache begrüßte Generalleutnant Kammhuber Finanzminister Ahrens als Vertreter des niedersächsischen Ministerpräsidenten Kopf, den Commander in chief des NATO-Abschnittes, dem das Geschwader im Herbst unterstellt wird, Landesbischof Jacobi und den Bischöflichen Offizial Prälat Grafenhorst, sowie weitere Persönlichkeiten des öffentlichen Lebens und Vertreter der alten und neuen Streitkräfte und der ausländischen Wehrmacht.

Generalleutnant Kammhuber dankte den vielen Stellen, die dazu beitrugen, daß der Termin für die Indienststellung des Geschwaders eingehalten werden konnte. Dem Land Niedersachsen für die Hilfe bei der Instandsetzung der Unterkünfte und des technischen Bereichs, der britischen Luftwaffe, die den Flugplatz nach der Zerstörung im Kriege wieder aufbaute, der „Canadair" für die rechtzeitige Zurverfügungstellung der Maschinen vom Typ Sabre VI und für die Ausbildung der Piloten in Kanada und Deutschland.

In Major Hartmann erhalte das Ge-

schwader einen Kommandore, der der Garant dafür sei, daß das JG 71 ein Mustergeschwader werde. Mit 352 Abschüssen sei er der erfolgreichste Jagdflieger der ganzen Welt und der einzige Träger des Ritterkreuzes mit Eichenlaub, Schwertern und Brillanten der neuen deutschen Wehrmacht. Die Aufgabe, die das Geschwader zu erfüllen habe, sei groß und verpflichtend. Es habe die Luftverteidigung Europas mit durchführen zu helfen. Bei den militärischen Maßnahmen gehe es darum, den Ausbruch eines Krieges vornherein zu verhindern. Darum müsse auch die Luftwaffe so ausgebildet werden, daß je- der potentielle Gegner im Angriff als Selbstmord erscheinen müsse und er ihn schon darum unterlasse. Der feste Wille der Bundeswehr, sich unter allen Umständen bis zum Äußersten zu verteidigen, erzeuge schon Abschreckung. „Darum sind wir auch bemüht, unserer Luftwaffe die besten Flugzeuge in die Hand zu geben. Jeder Soldat sei bereit, für die Ideale der freien Welt zu kämpfen und, wenn es sein müsse, auch sein Leben dafür einzusetzen. Von jeher sei die Kameradschaft bei den Fliegern vorbildlich gewesen. „Ich hoffe, Major Hartmann, daß der Geist auch in Ihrem Geschwader zum besten Vorbild emporsteigt."

Generalleutnant Kammhuber bat alle beteiligten Stellen, zu einer guten Einrichtung des Geschwaders und der weiteren

Ausstattung des Flugplatzes beizutragen: „Der Soldat, der seine Gesundheit und sein Leben für das Vaterland einsetzen soll, möchte kein Fremdkörper im Staate sein, sondern vom Vertrauen der Bevölkerung getragen werden. Nur dann kann er seine Aufgabe wirklich erfüllen!"

Nach der Indienststellung des Geschwaders intonierte das Musikkorps das Deutschlandlied. Noch während die angetretene Formationen abrückten, wurde eine Staffel des Geschwaders startklar gemacht, und zeigte dann in einem Schauflug in verschiedenen Formationen den hohen Leistungsstand der Maschinen und Piloten.

Newspaper clipping describing the day's festivities.

There is reason to celebrate the evening after becoming operational. One feels at home again.

The day after the ceremony the pilots relax and take it easy. The young pilots' level of self-confidence has risen. Here are the first "fighters" of JG 71. Sitting from right to left: Tuleweit, Hozmann, Meisterfeld, Carstensen, Empel, Poelchau, Rauzenberg and Gums. First row standing from right: Müller, Buss, Osmers, Meyer, Drube, Hartmann, Schmieder, Peters, Jansen, Harms. Top row from right: Namysio, Rack, Hülfert, Wallner, Batz.(BTM)

Despite all the frenzy, there is still time for a family life. Usch and Erich Hartmann in their garden with Ursula-Isabel, who is just learning how to walk.

Defense Minister Strauss conversing with members of the *Geschwader*. Left is Maj. Jäger, technical officer, right with the flight cap is the Kommodore, behind him Hptm. Pingel, commander of the *Nachrichteneinheit*.

USAF visit from Col. Jene Valencia, an American fighter ace with 23 victories.

During a visit to *Jagdgeschwader* 33 in Büchel, Hartmann meets with USAF Col. Toliver (center) and the Kommodore of *Jabo* 33, Walter Krupinski. The one-time enemies have become close friends.

Hartmann returns the visit at the U.S. 21st Fighter Squadron in Weathersfield, England. Next to Hartmann on the right is the commander of the American fighter squadron, Col. Ray Toliver, the later author of the book "Holt Hartmann vom Himmel" with his staff officers.

During a flight display by the USAF 21st Fighter Squadron. Hartmann in civilian clothing on the left, with the cigarette.

German-American friendship - fighter pilots past and present come together once more for a cheerful round. From left: Barkhorn, Valencia (USA), Neumann, Toliver (USA) and Hartmann.

Hartmann being visited by Col. Toliver at *Jagdgeschwader* 71 in 1961. The two are standing in front of a painted courier aircraft, a Piaggio, which served an important role in procuring spare parts and supplies.

Hartmann conversing with Canadian technical advisors. The relationship with the western Nato allies was always excellent.

An aircraft and the people who care for it. Left and rear is the refueling crew, right rear are the firemen. Standing in front of the airplane are, left, the technical director, on the right the Canadian technical advisor, in front of them on the left and right are maintenance, weapons, electronics, engine, airframe, radio and radar personnel and in the center foreground center is the pilot, Stuffz. Rack.

The first NATO gunnery competition for the 71st. Teams with their aircraft from the participating countries, from the foreground in the picture: Canadian, British, Norwegian, Italian and the Germans of the 71st.

The Hawker Hunter target aircraft acting as target tower, with the target flag in tow.

The evaluation. The hits on the flag are counted. Wearing the flight cap and with hands in pockets is Maj. Schmieder, teamleader of the German group. He is observing his shooters' results.

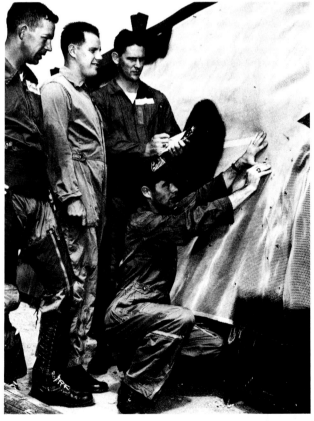

In the case of the Canadians, who were by far the victors, one can count entire groups of hits on the flag.

The Kommodore visits the gunnery team. Here in a serious conversation with one of his pilots, Rolf Batz.

The Canadian commander talks shop with Maj. Hartmann.

Hartmann together with his airbase comrade Werner Kaupisch (left) discusses the situation with the team commander Schmieder (second from left) and two of his pilots Namisio (center), and Rack next to him.

The first aircraft emergency net is tested at the *Geschwader*. The aircraft rolls into the steel netting, the upper cable slides over the cockpit, the pilot ducks instinctively.

With a thud, the steel cable cuts the canopy away and snags the airplane on the rear edge of the cockpit. If the pilot had not ducked, his head would be missing.

The first winter provided the *Geschwader* with a lot of trouble in the form of a frozen runway. The "Bubimat" is fabricated in the maintenance bay according to Hartmann's idea.

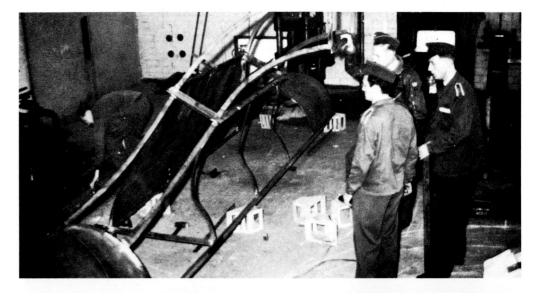

Here the "Bubimat" has already been attached to the engine like a giant vacuum cleaner, to that the hot gasses from the exhaust can be directed to the frozen surface of the runway.

The "Bubimat" is ready.

The "Bubimat" is towed into position.

Here, the "Bubimat" is in full operation. On the left, the de-iced runway, on the right the layer of ice is still compacted.

An overhead view of the "Bubimat" at work. After two hours, the runway was free of ice, and this allowed the *Geschwader* to be capable of operations even in the Winter.

A high-level visit at the *Geschwader*. The commanding General of the *Luftwaffengruppe* North, GenLt. Harlinghausen arrives.

The Commander of the French Air Force, Gen. Strehlin, visits the *Geschwader* and greets the unit commanders.

A squadron exchange with a Canadian squadron.

A visit to the *Geschwader* by foreign air force attaches from Bonn. Hartmann is fifth from the left.

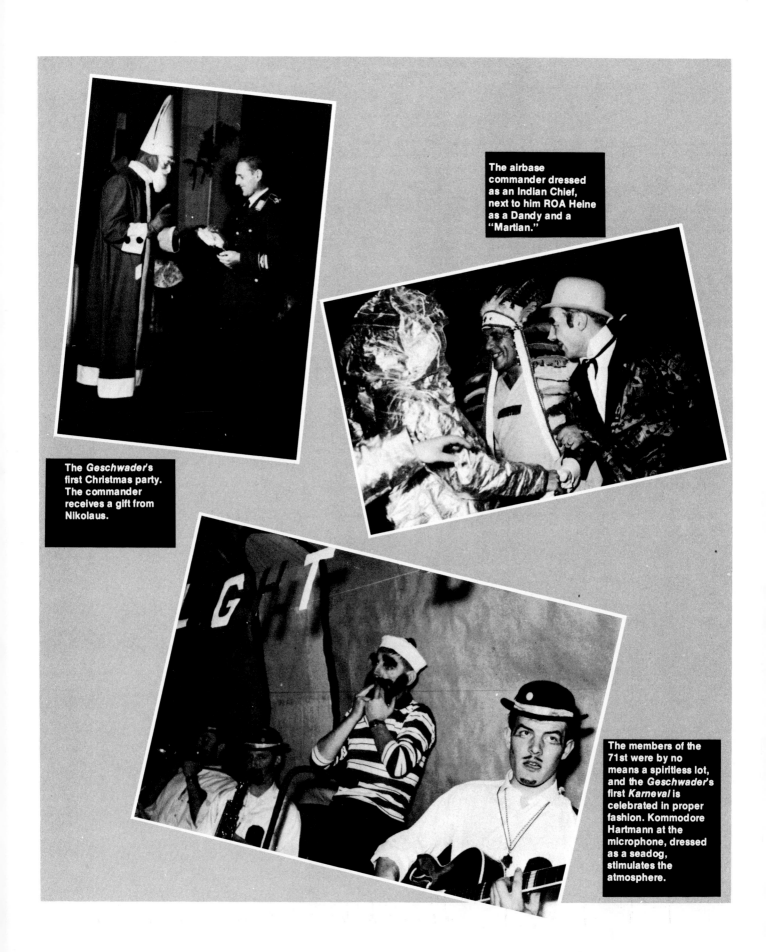

The airbase commander dressed as an Indian Chief, next to him ROA Heine as a Dandy and a "Martian."

The *Geschwader*'s first Christmas party. The commander receives a gift from Nikolaus.

The members of the 71st were by no means a spiritless lot, and the *Geschwader*'s first *Karneval* is celebrated in proper fashion. Kommodore Hartmann at the microphone, dressed as a seadog, stimulates the atmosphere.

AHLHORN JAGDGESCHWADER RECEIVES TRADITIONAL NAME

Newspaper article of the naming of Richthofen squadron on April 24 1961.

AHLHORN. April 21st 1961 became a great day for three *Geschwader*s of the Luftwaffe. On the occasion of Richthofen day and at the suggestion of Defense Minister Strauss *Jagdgeschwader* 71 from Ahlhorn, *Jagdgeschwader* 31 from Nörenich and the *Aufklärungsgeschwader* 51 (reconnaissance squadron) from Ingolstadt received honorific names in the tradition of the German Luftwaffe.

All the military traditions were being slowly revived. Here, a picture of the *Richthofenstaffel* with Manfred von Richthofen from World War I.

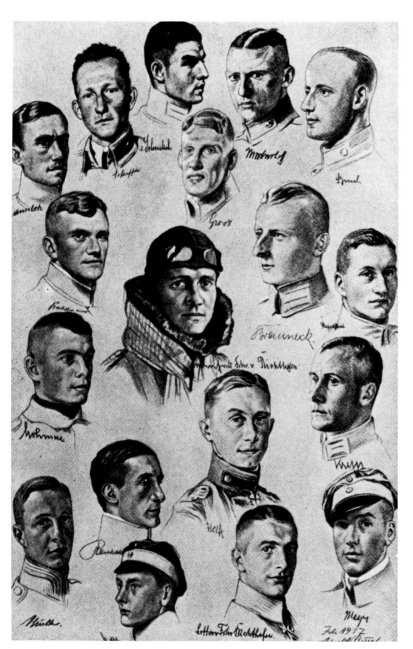

The festivities of this grand occasion, which took place before many representatives from public life, began with the marching in of the 3rd *Musikkorps* from Münster followed by the honor guard and the members of the *Geschwader*s. They continued with the reporting to the Kommodore by the *Geschwader* commanders, and as the most important portion of the award program the address by the *Inspekteur* of the Luftwaffe, Generalleutnant Kammhuber to the three *Geschwader*s.

The conversations of the people who appeared for the ceremony suddenly stopped when Gen.Lt. Kammhuber announced the honorific names for the three *Geschwader*s. The Ahlhorn *Jagdgeschwader* 71 was named for the famous airman Manfred von Richthofen.

This immortal pilot of the First World War was already a personality of leadership in his youth and served as a glowing example to all members of the Luftwaffe. The life of this young officer came to an end when he, whose spirit of attack carried his *Geschwader* to the highest level of performance, was killed through machine gun fire from the ground.

On 21 April 1961, on the anniversary of Richthofen's death, *Jagdgeschwader* 71 was renamed the *Richthofen Geschwader* and received this new squadron coat of arms. The NATO star with the traditional "R" of the old *Richthofenstaffel*.

At the same time, *Jabogeschwader* 31 and *Aufklärungsgeschwader* 51 received the honorifics "Boelcke" and "Immelmann." The three commanders during the conferment by the *Inspekteur* of the Luftwaffe. In the foreground from left to right: Kommodore Hartmann (Richthofen), Kommodore Barkhorn (Boelcke) and Kommodore Grasemann (Immelmann). On the stage from left to right: GenLt. Harlinghausen, Bolko Frhr. von Richthofen, a brother of Manfred von Richthofen, *Inspekteur General* Kammhuber and *General der Technik* Plocher.

There were two other pilots who forged the spirit of the Luftwaffe of the 1st World War: Hauptmann Oswald Boelcke and Oberleutnant Max Immelmann. The units bearing these honorifics, names just as obliging as that of Manfred von Richthofen, were *Jabo-Geschwader* 31 from Nörvenich and *Aufklärungsgeschwader* 51 from Ingolstadt.

The awarding of the armbands by Gen.Lt. Kammhuber was the most impressive scene of the festivities in Ahlhorn. The acceptance by the commanders of the *Geschwader*s, for the *Geschwader* Richthofen the world's most successful fighter pilot Oberstleutnant Hartmann, for the Boelcke *Geschwader* Oberst Barkhorn, and for the Immelmann *Geschwader* Oberstleutnant Grasemann, was a symbolic act for the entire German Luftwaffe. The high spirit of esprit de corps represented by these three names, is to be the guideline for all Luftwaffe members.

At the closing, all the day's participants were reminded of their duty to defend the unity of Germany by the playing of the German national anthem, jut as those pilots had, in whose names this day took place.

The *Inspekteur* of the Luftwaffe, General Kammhuber, awards the commanders representing their *Geschwader*s the new sleeve decoration bearing the honorific names.

The ceremonies have ended. A salute by the commanders Hartmann, Barkhorn and Grasemann and the German Luftwaffe can once more honor its ancestors.

Another souvenir photo of the big day. Bolko Frhr. von Richthofen, Hartmann and General Kammhuber.

A CASE FOR SHERLOCK HOLMES

Whenever there is something special going on in the West, the Soviets are not far. During the day of the ceremonies, a *Richthofen* guard noticed this car.

The "Richthofeners" made a report, and the squadron counter intelligence officer followed the car unnoticed and managed to photograph them. The Russians still haven't noticed anything, they have only run low of fuel during all their nosing about.

The gentlemen from the KGB still feel completely safe.

Suddenly the Soviet Colonel feels as though he's being observed as he comes out from paying, and his jaw literally drops open.

An embarrassed grin after recovering from the shock. Such men shy away from cameras and do not enjoy being found out.

NATO allies come more and more often for informational visits. Viewing the model of the airbase. To Hartmann's left is his old prisonmate Maj. Graf von der Schulenburg as the training officer of the *Richthofengeschwader*.

Viewing the repair facilities. To Hartmann's right is his Chief of Staff Hptm. Prahl.

Spain donated a Bf 109 to the German Museum in Munich. Prof. Willi Messerschmitt conducts the address during the festivities.

Prof. Messerschmitt conversing with his old chief test pilot Wendel, the long-time holder of the world speed record in a "Bf 109 R", in the center is Gen. Kammhuber.

Old Bf 109-flyers view their "Beule" once more. From left to right: Oberst (ret.) Josef Priller, Messerschmitt test pilot Wendel, and Hartmann.

The "Richthofeners" don't care to dance to marching music — they prefer a quick tempo. The commander accompanies.

The "Flight Band" of the *Geschwader* makes its first appearance here.

Daily routine in the *Geschwader*. Morning briefing with the pilots. Front row from the left: Kommodore Hartmann, *Staffelkapitän* Müller, a Canadian Captain, the Kommodore of the airbase Kaupisch, behind Kaupisch is Hptm. Erlemann, who later became the commander of the *Mölders Geschwader*, and today is the Luftwaffe Adjutant in Washington.

At the end of the duty day, a stop at the bar for a glass of beer. From the right: Hptm. Harms, Herr Schulze-König, Kommodore Hartmann, Hptm. Werner, Maj. Hohagen, who also a seasoned pilot and Hartmann's one-time flight instructor.

An F-84 in a pilot's sights.

An F-104 Starfighter in the sights.

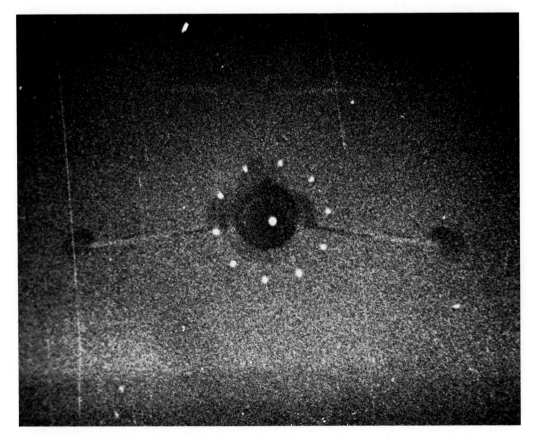

A German Luftwaffe fact-finding group was sent to the USA to look at American air bases. From left to right: Maj. Hartmann, Otl. Koch, Oberst Strümpell, Oberst Siebert, Oberst Hoffmann, BrigGen. von Plötz, Otl. Schröder, Oberst Vogel, Oberst Hauser, Oberst Dr. Roos.

They are received in the U.S. by 3-star General Lee (center). Hartmann stands to the outside left.

Robert Lee, a WWII pilot and USAF General, and Maj. Hartmann had long talks about the Starfighter and were of the same opinion.

The American 4-star General Kuter, commander of NORAD is presented with the old coat of arms of the *Richthofengeschwader.*

Maj. Hartmann and
Brig.Gen. v. Plötz
surrounded by American
air cadets during a visit to
the Maxwell Academy in
the U.S.

There were long talks
between young and old,
the cadets were quite
hungry for knowledge.
Here, the cadet
spokesman and Col. Ray
Toliver (left) with Maj.
Hartmann.

An American cadet
proudly shows Hartmann
his ring. It is the symbol
of a graduate of the best
American air academy.

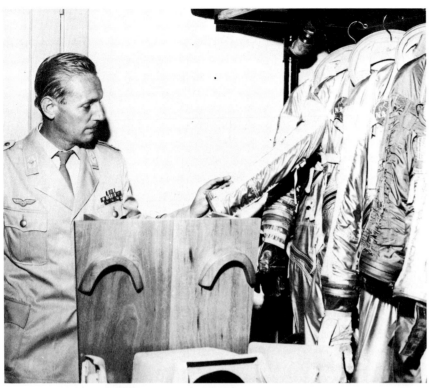

Hartmann in the dressing room of the astronauts. He is feeling a space suit made from a very costly material.

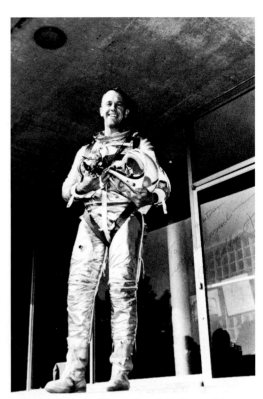

Astronaut Alan B. Shepard sent Hartmann this photo to as a souvenir.

The test chair for the astronauts. Hartmann, left.

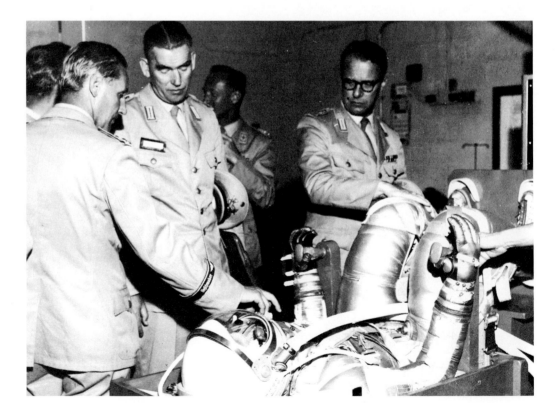

Alan Shepard talks with Hartmann and Gen. v. Plötz (left). Oberst Siebert and Otl. Koch strain to listen to the "pilot-English," or jargon.

A briefing at NASA. From right: Brig.Gen. v. Plötz, Hartmann, Otl. Schröder, Oberst Sieber, Oberst Dr. Roos and Otl. Koch.

Hartmann views the F-105 heavy fighter-bomber with great interest. Robert Johnson, in the white suit and himself a WWII fighter ace, explains the technology.

The cockpit gets Hartmann's undivided attention. Which new type of electronics where to be installed here, and for what purpose? Robert Johnson explains.

During this trip Hartmann was allowed to fly along on any type aircraft he desired, except the F-104 Starfighter. Here prior to a flight in the F-106, which was the standard interceptor in the U.S. Hartmann and his U.S. pilot during the pre-flight inspection.

"Please climb aboard sir" says the young USAF Captain.

The F-106 was a superior aircraft. Easily accessible from all points for maintenance, it was a delta-wing aircraft with great range, held and altitude record, handled well and was super fast. Hartmann standing up on the left during the inspection.

Hand positions and movements are carefully observed while strapping into the ejection seat.

A last wave and the super-bird taxis out to the runway.

After their return Hartmann gives a satisfied smile. It was an outstanding flight, almost twice as high as the Starfighter without even using afterburner. Mach 2 was reached with ease, completely automatic target search and lock-on, it was utterly superior.

Having returned, the aircraft "changing of the guard" began. Old and new meet in the air. In the foreground is the good old Sabre 6, next to it the first Starfighter of the *Waffenschule* (weapons school).

The "*Unglücksrabe*" (lit. unlucky raven) on the ground (here a two seat trainer version).

Jagdgeschwader Richthofen held an open house on June 18 1961, which, due to heavy rains, was not successful.

The "Nike Hercules" standard air defense missile.

AIRSHOWS

There was a lot for curious spectators to see. This is a one-man life raft which is stored a fighter aircraft's ejection seat as a cushion.

Various small arms used by the Luftwaffe. In the foreground is the old famous MG 42, which was among the standard issued weapons in WWII.

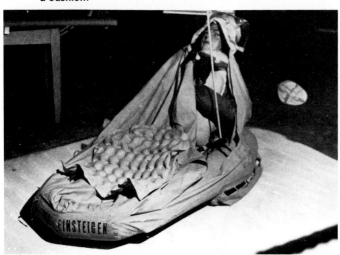

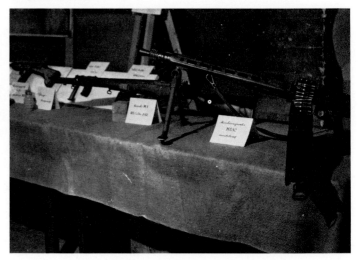

A training and courier airplane, the Piaggio P 149 D.

An amphibious air/sea rescue Grumman HU 16 C of the German Marine (Navy).

The Bundeswehr's (armed forces) first generation cargo aircraft, a Noratlas Nora 2501.

A naval reconnaissance and attack aircraft belonging to the Marine, an Armstrong Withworth Seahawk MK 101.

German naval aviation's first anti-submarine warfare aircraft: Fairey Gannet ASMK 4.

The Luftwaffe's jet trainer and light tactical fighter: Fouga Magister CM 170 R.

The standard fighter-bomber of the Luftwaffe's first generation aircraft, the Thunderstreak F-84 F.

The second generation aircraft of the Bundesluftwaffe is represented by the Starfighter F-104 G.

The British air demonstration team "Red Arrows" with their Hawker Hunters, the standard British fighter of the period.

The Italian air demonstration team in formation flight over the Ahlhorn airfield.

Clear view of an Orenda engine, which was installed in the Canadair Sabre MK VI.

The precise interval between aircraft demonstrated by the Italians is an indication of the high degree of skill demanded by such flying.

Hartmann, having been transferred to the *Luftwaffenamt* (Office of the Luftwaffe) in Cologne-Wahn, now directs the tactical inspections of operational units. Here he is waiting with colleagues at the Cologne-Wahn airfield for a flight to one of the *Luftwaffe Geschwaders*.

The transport aircraft "Noratlas" has arrived, and the inspection team composed of representatives from all air force skills is complete: Hartmann, the team chief, is sixth from the right.

Hartmann at a reception having a stimulating conversation with the French Air Force attache Colonel Wirth (right) and with Col. Ray Toliver, USAF (center).

Two generations of flyers meet for Herbert Eklöh's 65th birthday celebration. From left: "Flying Father" Schulte, Gen. (ret.) Galland, Captain Hanna Reitsch, Herbert Eklöh and Hartmann.

Former enemies meet in
Baden-Baden. From left:
Robert Stanford-Tuck,
British flying ace,
Hartmann and Galland.

A birthday reception for
Theo Bennecke,
president of the German
Air and Space Society.

At Theo Bennecke's
reception, Hartmann is on
the left in a conversation
with the first man on the
moon, Neil Armstrong,
and Rudi Schlitt.

An interview and briefing in the USA about issues concerning air force reserves.

Departure from the USA and Oberst Hartmann's last official trip.

Opposite: June 1970, visiting the American Air Force Reserves in the U.S. Hartmann is third from the right. On the outside left is the German television moderator Woller, from the ZDF network.

30 September 1970. The new "BO 20" career law allows jet pilots of 40 years and older to voluntarily separate from active service. Gen. Hempel, Chief of Staff of the Luftwaffe, conducts the retirement of personnel. To his left is Oberst Hartmann.

Erich Hartmann and his old war-time commander, Gen. Diether Hrabak, separate from the Luftwaffe on the same day, at their request, and say good-bye to one another.

HARTMANN RESIGNS FROM SERVICE

Bonn (UPI) - Luftwaffe Oberst Erich ("Bubi") Hartmann, who as a fighter pilot in the Second World War shot down 352 enemy aircraft and has since been considered the world's leading fighter ace, wants to retire from active service on 30 September 1970. Hartmann, who spent ten years as prisoner of war of the Soviets, is 48 years old. Currently, Hartmann, who was awarded the Oak Leaves and Swords with Diamonds to the Knight's Cross of the Iron Cross, works in the Office of the Luftwaffe. Hartmann possesses all qualifications of a pilot of a modern jet fighter.

The last flight before retirement: Adieu, Luftwaffe!

The last day in uniform, Erich and Usch Hartmann.

Hartmann, now a pensioner, with his family.

In Civilian Dress
Once and For All

After 30 years, Hartmann is a civilian once again and obviously feels quite well. Here he has "Baron Snoopy" pursue an F-86 for the reporters.

Memories while looking at his war-time award.

The personal retirement gift of the pilots of the *Luftflotte*, of which Hartmann is particularly proud, an orange flight suit with the unit crests of all the operational *Geschwaders*. He is pointing to the crest of his *Richthofen-Geschwader*.

276

Barely a civilian again and American pilots of WWII called him to a meeting of pilots in St. Louis. From left the second honored guest General Tomatsu Yokoyama, Leo Volkmer, a U.S. combat pilot and originator of the meeting, Hartmann and U.S. General James H. Howard, Washington D.C.

Thousands of Americans visit the international Pilots' Convention in St. Louis and view the aircraft from the Second World War.

The old Messerschmitt Bf 108 had to be there as well, only the markings were incorrect.

277

In the evening, the hosts and guests meet in the hotel's banquet hall. From the left: the host Leo Volkmer with his wife Jane and General Yokoyama with his wife.

The other side of the head table with Erich Hartmann and his wife Usch and the American WWII Pilot Paul Prokowski with his wife.

Hartmann as a guest speaker. Next to him is Bob Hoover, the most famous American test pilot and aerobat, he was also a fighter pilot during the Second World War, flying the P-51 Mustang.

278

Hartmann Has Been Completely
Reestablished in the U.S. Headlines

COMBAT PILOTS: World War II pilots gathered here to reminisce (from left) are: Gen. Glennon Moran, St. Louis; Japanese Gen. Tomatsu Yokoyama; George Gay of the United States Navy and German ace Col. Erich Hartmann. (Post-Dispatch Photo)

Hartmann during an interview on American television, photographed from the TV screen.

World War II Pilots Hold Grand Reunion

Col. Erich Hartmann was talking about fighter pilots and World War II.

"They, we, are all the same," said the German credited with downing 352 Allied aircraft in the war. "They are young, like to fly and they don't think too much politically."

He stopped a moment, ran his hand through the hair that tabbed him as the Blond Knight of Germany. More than a quarter of a century after World War II, he had additional

thoughts on that war.

"There was politics and we didn't think much about it then," he said. "Afterward we found that the war was not necessary."

Weekend Meeting

Hartmann, now on duty with the West German Air Force, is one of scores of World War II combat pilots who have gathered in St. Louis this weekend for a convention. Besides Hartmann, former Japanese Maj. Gen. Tomatsu Yokoyama

is in St. Louis. Yokoyama commanded a Zero fighter squadron in the Philippines. That squadron downed 350 allied aircraft.

Hartmann; Yokoyama, now a business man; George H. Gay, the only survivor of United States Navy Torpedo Squadron 8 at the Battle of Midway and Gen. Glennon Moran of St. Louis sat on a sofa at the Sheraton-Jefferson Hotel talking about the old times. Moran was a fighter pilot with the

Eighth Air Force in World War II and is now with the Air National Guard.

Both Agree

When pressed on the point that the young now apparently do think politically, Gay interjected: "Only those that get the publicity."

Hartmann turned and said softly. "That's right."

All but seven of Hartmann's air victories were scored on the Eastern Front and he spent 10 years in Russian prisons after World War II. His wife, who came to the convention with him, said that those were the worst years.

"In the war he was able to come home about 10 days every three months," she said. "But afterward, we did not know if he would be released. It was living day to day for 10 years. That was the hardest."

Sept - 8 - 1970

Reunited as Friends

COL. ERICH HARTMANN, left, Germany's super-ace who shot down 352 allied aircraft during World War II, talks with retired Gen. James H. Howard of Washington, D.C., who won the Medal of Honor for downing several German fighters. The two were among several allied and enemy fliers who attended a reunion in St. Louis Sunday.

Attends U.S. Reunion

German Fighter Pilot Most Popular Fellow

ST. LOUIS (AP)—Col. Erich Hartmann, the World War II German fighter pilot credited with downing 352 enemy aircraft, attended a reunion of American fighter pilots and crews this weekend and found himself signing scores of autographs.

"He's the ace of all aces," said Chester Klier, 48, of Florissant, Mo., who piloted a B26 bomber in raids over Germany. "He was an enemy of mine, but I hold him in high esteem."

In Klier's scrapbook, Hartmann wrote: "Forget the bad times and look forward to the good times."

Hartmann and his wife, Ursula, watched a U.S. Air Force film Saturday night showing destruction rained on Germany by Allied planes.

"WE SEE NOW it was a mistake," Hartmann said of the war.

"We are through two wars. Our children can go around and visit all the places in the world and make friends. If people can understand each other, they can understand the problems.

"Young people today don't like wars. They don't even like the military service. I can understand that."

Most of Hartmann's kills

were on the Russian front. He flew some 1,400 combat missions, was never wounded, but had to bail out or make forced landings several times.

Trim and athletic-looking at 48, Hartmann was one of the few among 400 persons attending the reunion who looked as if he could still fly combat missions. After the war, he spent more than 10 years in a Russian prison. Since his release in 1955 he has been an officer in the West German Air Force. He will retire Oct. 1.

ONE OTHER former enemy pilot attended, Maj. Gen. Tomotsu Yokoyama. He commanded a squadron of 50 Japanese Zero fighters over the Philippines which was credited with destroying 350 Allied aircraft. Retired at 62, Yokoyama is an aircraft historian and an expert on the restoration of planes.

"He's lucky to still be alive," said Peter Keith, 54, of St. Louis, who flew a Navy Hellcat in the same area as Yokoyama. "He led the attack on Clark Field north of Manila," said Keith. "They hurt Gen. Douglas MacArthur's troops pretty bad."

The reunion, billed as the "first and last," was organized by Don "Baron" Volkmer, head of a Dallas manufacturing firm. He flew combat missions in the Battle of the Bulge.

An air show Sunday at nearby Alton, Ill., featured such World War II vintage planes as the P-51, Messerschmitt, T6 trainer, Lightning P38, Corsair, Hellcat and Spitfire.

****

Combat aces from three countries buried the hatchet Sunday at a reunion in St. Louis. From left: Maj. Gen. Tamotsu Yokoyama of Japan; Don Volkmer of Dallas, who organized the reunion; Col. Erich Hartman of Germany, and Gen. James H. Howard of Washington, D. C.

Hartmann pages through an American printing of the book about him, which appeared in 1970 under the title, ''The Blond Knight of Germany.''

In May 1971 Hartmann was invited to the United States once again for various occasions. Here he is with Leo Volkmer and wife again.

Also invited were the British fighter pilot Peter Townsend and his wife. Here he is sitting in the cockpit of an old Spitfire. Hartmann is on the right, Leo Volkmer on the left.

Erich Hartmann in front of a "modified" Bf 109. It came from Spanish inventory, has a Rolls Royce Merlin engine (like its former rival the Spitfire) and was outfitted as it is seen here for a film: with the coat of arms of III/JG 27 (and the *Grünherz* of JG 54).

An exchange of experiences and a viewing of the McDonnell-Douglas works in St. Louis. Here in front of the first German Phantom fighter-bomber are, from left: Peter Townsend, Dick Matheis, Hartmann and Leo Volkmer.

Hartmann and Peter Townsend dig up old memories. A television interview in Dallas, Texas.

Peter Townsend and
Erich Hartmann in the
Gemini space capsule.

In the summer of 1971
American friends Wylene
and Frank Buzze came to
Cologne to visit the
Hartmann's, their first
reunion in 14 years. Here
in front of the *Kölner Dom*
with Usch Hartmann.

Even Bob Hoover, the
famous test pilot, came
for a visit and greets Erich
Hartmann.

Hartmann was taken in by sport flying even while serving in the Bundeswehr. Here with Gen. Galland as the winner of the *Krähenflug* in Braunschweig in 1967 in a conversation with the President of the Braunschweig Aeroclub, Heinz Nitsche.

A non-flying get-together of the "hunters," shooting clay pigeons in Burgstein/Westfalen. From left: Erich Hartmann, Walter Krupinski and Dieter Hrabak.

Erich Hartmann with his daughter in front of the main building of the Nordrhein-Westfalen flight school. Hartmann stayed loyal to flying here even after his retirement as a flight instructor and training director.

Flight around Germany in 1967 with Gen. Galland as pilot and Hartmann as navigator. Here, they are studying the charts in front of Galland's airplane.

On Wasserkuppe hill with the light plane builder Schleicher from Poppenhausen before a test flight of a new construction.

An autograph for a flying enthusiast on Wasserkuppe.

An instructor must pay particular attention to ensure his student follows the pre-flight check list exactly.

One of the last "Fieseler Störche" airplanes from WWII is given a test flight before being sent to the United States.

The observation point for instructors and students during flight training.

Every Sunday morning the "old eagles" of the Hangelar flight school meet, here with Erich Hartmann (right). Next to him is the director of the school, Helmut Halfmann.

Shortly before leaving Hangelar and finally moving to Weil im Schönbuch/ Württemberg. Usch and Erich and an "old eagle."

Hartmann's home airfield is that of the Ammerbuch flying club at Poltringen near his hometown of Weil im Schönbuch, where Hartmann has lived since 1973.

Here is the runway of the special Poltringen airfield between Herrenberg and Tübingen, ideally framed by the forest area of Schönbuch in the background.

In June of 1976 there was another big airshow at the Poltringen airfield with an "Oldtimer Show", and many interested people visited.

Here the "Oldtimers" are formed up on the airfield for viewing. In the foreground is a reproduction of a Klemm 35, fully aerobatic.

Hartmann in front of the hangar between pilots of the club who are casting a critical eye skyward to see if the weather will hold. Standing on the right is the director of the Ammerbuch Luftsportgruppe at Tübingen and a former "Wilde Sau" fighter pilot, Wilhelm Greiner.

The old Focke-Wulf Fw 44 Stieglitz trainer.

The old U.S. "Moul" trainer was also there.

Here is the corresponding British trainer, the DeHavilland "Tiger Moth."

Not to be overlooked is the old training glider "SG 38" with "old eagle" Oskar Pflaumer.

One of the first pre-war German trainer aircraft with an enclosed cockpit, the old Bücker Bü 181.

The good, old 7-cylinder radial engine SH 14 of the Focke-Wulf "Stieglitz."

Even the *Oberbürgermeister* of Herrenberg, Heinz Schroth (center) and the *Ortsvorsteher* of Gültstein und Kauh, Willi Hirth, who is also a glider pilot, visited the "Old Timer Show" with Erich Hartmann (left).

Hartmann prior to take-off with a student to introduce him to controlled clear-weather flying (C-VFR).

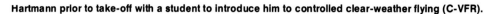

290

Erich Hartmann with his wife Usch during a pleasant visit to the Poltringen airfield.

Hartmann teaches flight theory during ground school during a hot July 1976 conducted under ancient linden trees. Erich Hartmann is on the chair, to his left Kurt Egeler and Rudi Bockhorn.

AIRPLANE CHRISTENING

We have come here today to christen the new Rhein-Main flying club airplane. At first glance, this may not appear to be unusual, because the christening of an airplane was, and probably still is today, somewhat of a tradition. I say "probably still is today" because it seems to be the "up to date" thing to do to break with tradition. It is also currently accepted as "progressive", in keeping with today's vernacular, to only speak from reason and dismiss emotion as conservative. But I believe that emotion is an essential elixir of human life, and I am prepared to be called a conservative by those who disagree with this notion. I am certain, however, that today's christening

Der Rhein-Main Fliegerclub e. V. gibt sich die Ehre

zur Taufe der Flugzeuge D-EGEV und D-ENEI auf die Namen
Erich Hartmann und Karl Dernbach
einzuladen.

Die Taufe findet am 24. März 1973, um 10 Uhr im Flugplatzhotel „Bimbes" auf dem Flugplatz Egelsbach statt. Anschließend bitten wir Sie zu einem kleinen Imbiß.

Invitation to Egelsbach for a "Fuji" sport airplane christening in the name of Erich Hartmann.

breaks with tradition and is unusual because the man for whom the airplane is to be named is an unusual man. I am speaking of Erich Hartmann. And it is not possible to give a clear answer to the question "Why Erich Hartmann?" Not just an answer for us here, but a statement for everyone. Even for those who do not ask this question.

And this answer, this statement, I give freely. Influenced by no man. Including the club director. Freely, as a young pilot and member of the so-called "post-war generation", who has not only examined the past but also the present and still gives this answer. It would be cheap to say that we want to christen this airplane in honor of Erich Hartmann as the world's leading fighter pilot. That means looking merely at his function as a soldier and not his qualities as a man. It may be that it is easy to fall in with the indifferent tone of language about the so-called coping with the past. It is my opinion however, that one gets an incomplete picture of the past - has a one-sided attitude toward the past when one only condemns crimes (and when I say "only", this doesn't mean that I do not consider it necessary to do so) and conceals the values of humanity, integrity and courage with the comfortable cloak of silence.

We, however, have the courage not only to recognize these human qualities, but also to uphold them. Because these qualities are still completely valid.

One of those people who stand for such qualities and who embody them still is Erich Hartmann.

In their book "Holt Hartmann vom Himmel", the American Ray Toliver, a former active duty officer and test pilot of the U.S. Air Force, and the writer Trevor Constable have described Erich Hartmann far better than I am able to here.

One review of the book has the following sentence: "This is a report about a phenomenon by the name of Erich Hartmann. It might well be the fate of human phenomena to not be seen as such in their own time. It is left to history to report about much later, to pass on the qualities achieved by this phenomenon, although these qualities were extremely necessary to the times in which they were created.

History gives more than enough examples of these flagrant human oversights, which have their origins in envy, resentment and ignorance. It is not our desire to assume the position of intellectual elite who are way ahead of their time by saying that, for us, Erich Hartmann is such a human phenomenon. We offer this as an example to clarify our decision.

Our only desire is to orient ourselves to the values which Erich Hartmann has upheld. This means nothing more, and nothing less, than to identify with him entirely as a man.

As a man who has demonstrated much courage in more than 800 aerial dogfights. Even when he was simply forced to be courageous just to survive.

As a man who declined an order to return home, because it was inconceivable to him to leave his compatriots alone on the front. As a man who not only pursued spectacular victories in aerial combat but whose primary concern was to bring his inexperienced wingman home again.

As a man whose character so disciplined his flying temperament that he was capable of spectacular feats.

As a man who refused to follow an order sending him to safety, so that he, relying only on his own powers, could help defenseless civilian refugees, women and children. A decision which cost him eleven years of his life. As a man who throughout eleven years of the most horrible terror and despotic acts could not betray his own integrity and personality.

As a man who, after his release summoned up so much physical and spiritual energies as to pass the ruthless jet pilot certification test with distinction.

As a man who, as the commander of the first German Jet

Erich Hartmann christens the "Fuji" with a glass of champagne.

Fighter *Geschwader* looked after the pilot development and training with proverbial esprit de corps.

As a man who excluded himself from a career through his openness and honesty and left it to perhaps less qualified, but more diplomatic men.

A man who has always displayed his integrity and courage when it came to calling a spade a spade. And this is unpleasant, as it often is for such men, and often carries more than temporary drawbacks.

As a man who, at his own request, climbed out of the cockpits of super-sonic jets in order to climb into the considerably more modest cockpits of sport aviation. At the end of their book, Toliver and Constable write: "Erich Hartmann voluntarily retired from active service. Not as a man who survived his own legend, but as a man who had preserved the measure for striking a proper balance in a time of changing values." I think this measure is one which doesn't seek human confrontation, but human cooperation. A measure bound with sovereignty, which reigns in and disciplines his flying temperament.

A measure by which every man must critically measure himself, and not only when it comes to flying an airplane.

A measure which permits no daring gambles, which much more lets the wonderful experience of flying be borne by a sense of responsibility.

A measure which does not permit elitist snobbery, but rather promotes human courtesy.

A measure which demands the levelling of hierarchical or social differences.

A measure in which honesty and openness are crucial,

After the christening, a toast to many wonderful flights and happy landings of the *Erich Hartmann*.

because dishonesty can have catastrophic consequences.

A measure that flying is not for ego-building.

We do not want to transpose this measure of a man which contains all these characteristics on the technical instrument of the airplane itself, but rather on those people who want to flying this new airplane.

That is why the name Erich Hartmann stands on the new airplane of the Rhein-Main flying club.

Life of Oberst a.D. (retired) Erich Hartmann

19 April 1922	Born in Weissach, Kreis Leonberg, Württemberg. Parents: Dr. (med.) Alfred Hartmann, general practitioner, (died 1952) and Elisabeth Hartmann, nee Machtholf
1924-1928	With his parents in China. His father had established a general practice in Changsha
1928	Return to Germany
1928-1932	Volksschule (elementary school) in Weil im Schönbuch
1933-1940	Oberschule (similar to a U.S. high school) in Böblingen, Rottweil and Korntal
1940	In the early portion, graduated high school. -Since 1936, sailplane *Gruppe*, first in Weil im Schönbuch, then in Korntal. Exams completed: *A, B, C* (pilots' license) in 1939 on the Klippeneck (Schwabian Alps) near Spaichingen.
10 Oct 1940	Voluntarily entered the Luftwaffe; induction into *Ausbildungs-Regiment* 10 (training regiment) in Neukuhr/Ostpreussen
March 1941	*Fahnenjunker-Gefreiter; Luftkriegsschule* II (air combat school) at Berlin-Gatow
August 1941	Final examination, military pilots' license B 2 (LKS II)
Oct 1941 - Feb 1942	*Jagdflieger-Vorschule* (fighter pilot prep school) II at Lachen Speyerdorf, Rheinland-Pfalz
Feb 1942 - Jul 1942	*Jagdfliegerschule* (fighter pilots' school) II Zerbst-Anhalt
Jul 1942 - Oct 1942	*Ergänzungsgruppe Ost*, Gleiwitz/Oberschlesien
Oct 1942 - May 1943	7th/III JG 52 (Eastern front)
May 1943 - Aug 1943	*Staffelführer* (squadron leader) of 7/III JG 52
Aug 1943 - Oct 1944	*Staffelkapitän* of 9/III JG 52
Oct 1944 - Nov 1944	7/III JG 52, *Staffelführer* and deputy commander of the *Gruppe*
Dec 1944 - Jan 1945	Commander, I/JG 53
From Feb 1945,	Commander of I/JG 52 until the end of the war. A four-week temporary duty in March 1945 at the *Versuchsgruppe* (test group) 262 (Me 262 jet fighter) at Lechfeld, after which back to I/JG 52
May 8 1945	Surrender at Pisek, Czechoslovakia; taken by an American tank division
May 25 1945	Handed over to the Russians as a prisoner of war
July 1945	Transported: Budweis - Budapest - Marmarasiged -Kiev - Smolensk - Moscow - Jaroslavel -Vologda - Kirov; there accommodation at the moor camp in Kirov (type of work: cutting peat)
Aug 1945 - Oct 1945	Moor-camp at Kirov
Oct 1945 - Oct 1947	KGF-camp, Gryazovets
Oct 1947 - Oct 1949	KGF-camp, Cherepovets
Oct 1949 - Dec 1949	KGF-camp, Ivanovka (1st trial)
Dec 1949 - May 1950	GPU prison, Ivanovo
May 1950 - Nov 1950	KZ camp Shachtu (2nd trial)
Nov 1950 - May 1952	GPU camp Novotsherkaask
May 1952 - Nov 1952	KZ camp Asbest
Nov 1952 - Aug 1954	KZ prison camp Degtyarka
Aug 1954 - Oct 1954	GPU prison Sverdlovsk
Oct 1954 - Oct 1955	GPU prison Novotsherkaask
15 Oct 1955	Released to go home as a result of Bundeskanzler Adenauer's visit to Moscow
Fall, 1956	Entered the Luftwaffe of the Bundesrepublik. - Renewed flight training: on the T-6 until early 1957 in Landsberg, then on the T-33 in Fürstenfeldbruck until July 1957, then in the USA until December 1957: gunnery training at Luke Air Force Base.
Jan 1958 - Jan 1959	Operations officer at WSdLw 10 in Oldenburg
Jan 1959 - Jun 1962	Commander, JG 71 "Richthofen", Ahlhorn/Oldenburg
until Oct 1970	LwA/InKpfVbdLw
Oct 1970	Retired from active duty

Married since September of 1944; one son born 1945, died in 1948; one daughter born in February 1957